You Won't Be Coming Back

You Won't Be Coming Back

To you who read this —
Best wishes from a grateful
heart ~
  may your dreams lead you
to a memorable history of
your own ~

Beverly Finn

2-9-'14

Beverly Finn

To order additional copies of this book, contact:
Xlibris LLC
1-888-795-4274
www.Xlibris.com
Orders@Xlibris.com
118827

-CONTENTS-

Part II: Glenwood City and River Falls

Part III: Life in Illinois

DEDICATION

Dedicated to my sister Gladie, for her continuing bravery and resilience in dealing with the many adversities in her life.

Dedicated also to my sister Irene, whose life was forever altered.

Child abuse casts a shadow the length of a lifetime. When people speak out about it, we can perhaps help others who are mistreated or abused to get out of that shadow and into the sunlight.

IN MEMORIAM

Beloved son, Brian Michael Finn (May 4, 1967-February 17, 2010)

Also in remembrance of Erin SiLei Finn, beloved granddaughter (born March 26, 2008), whisked halfway round the world and out of our lives at the same time our son was lost to us.

Part I: Cadott

INTRODUCTION

Words that carry the weight of destiny are never forgotten. Not forgotten, either, are the voices and the people who deliver those words.

The brightness of the cool October day spilled over into the east-facing home ec room and onto my sewing table as I worked on my newest project, a turquoise pinwale corduroy jumper. It would be just right, I thought, with a blouse or sweater underneath, for the days ahead. With its high midriff, straps that crossed in back, and the gored and flared skirt, it would flatter my eighteen-inch waist.

Firm, authoritative steps came down the wooden hallway, paused briefly, and then entered our third-hour classroom. I glanced up then resumed my work on the garment I had chosen to sew. No need for me to worry, I thought. As a good student, I never got in trouble in school.

PRINCIPAL'S
MESSAGE

As another school year is about to be given its place in history I should like to ask this question of all the students of Cadott High School: "Have you contributed to the best of your ability toward making this a better community, state, country, and world in which to live; and have you personally taken advantage of all your opportunities for self-improvement?" If you can answer "Yes" to this question, may I extend my congratulations for a task well done. If your answer is "No," do not be discouraged, but rather encouraged, for another opportunity for good is still available to you if at this time you determine to answer "Yes" the next time this question is asked of you.

N. F. Panzenhagen

Mr. Panzenhagen, our principal at Cadott High School, came right for me, though, his rugged and solemn face revealing that he was here for serious business. We all respected and liked Mr. Panzenhagen even though we often called him "Old Pants Are Hangin'" among ourselves.

Looking me straight in the eyes, Mr. Panzenhagen said the words that would come to be the single most defining moment in my life: "Beverly, gather all your things because you won't be coming back."

Panicked, heart beating fast, fear and disbelief overwhelmed me. How could this be? This was my school. Had been since I was six years old. I belonged here. I had finally gotten to be a frontline majorette in the all-girls' marching group, the Hornettes. How could I not be coming back?

Fumbling fingers and trembling hands and a desperate disbelief hindered me as I cleaned out all my sewing items from my drawer, trying to carefully fold the tissue-paper pattern pieces into their envelope and to scoop up the fabric, scissors, pin cushion, and other items I used in that room.

No chance to say good-bye to Jeanne or my other friends. I hoped that they would understand that it wasn't my idea to leave without a proper farewell and that I didn't want to leave them.

On to my locker, nervously dealing with something beyond my control. Where was I going? I didn't deal well with the unknown. I always moved my hands in a quick, fluttering movement at my sides near my thighs in excitement or anxiety-producing situations like this, which was frustrating for my mother. She didn't understand why I did that and tried, unsuccessfully over the years, to get me to stop. I had seen my mother and grandmother react nervously to unsettling situations, and I had the same trait, which manifested itself now.

Mr. Panzenhagen escorted my sister Ruby and me from our much-loved school to the outside where our social worker, Mrs. Grace W., was waiting to take us home to pack our things. Our brothers, Ken and Ed, had already been taken from their classrooms beforehand, evidently, because they did not come with us at that time.

I didn't want to go with Mrs. W. and sassed her all the way home, even though I ordinarily was well behaved. I was angry and upset and dealing with a traumatic incident a kid shouldn't have to deal with. Her retort to me: "Why, you impudent little snip!" This was said with full exasperation, frustration, and anger.

Having a good understanding of verbal and vocabulary skills, I knew exactly what she meant. Even as a young person, I knew that her professional demeanor was inappropriate—I was a kid being taken out of the only home I'd ever known, after all.

I don't remember simmering down, but I must have, at least enough to hear and understand her instructions to me: "Pack your things because you're leaving here."

My mother gave us each a brown paper grocery bag for our few meager belongings: a couple of dresses, a slip, and some underwear and socks could all fit in. I was wearing the only coat I had, made of black woolen tweed with red trim that I had bought with my babysitting money from Marita, who lived next-door. No extra shoes, no personal items at all. No time to remember to climb into the attic to get the bride doll Miss Freese had lovingly given me in fifth grade because she knew that I had never had a doll, or the small American Beauty doll my mother had given me that had been packaged in a box of Fab laundry detergent.

"Come on! We need to get going!"

So after a tearful farewell to our mother, we went into the car again to be driven in silence to our destiny that Wednesday in October 1957.

The Froggatts were foster parents in a holding home (or whatever they were called back then) in Chippewa Falls, a larger town than Cadott and thirteen miles to the west. Foster parents took in damaged or at-risk children and did their best (in most cases) to help turn them around and make their lives better. The house, big and imposing, was at the southwest side of the city near Lake Hallie. The long, enclosed porch wrapped across the front of the house on the north side and echoed when we walked across it.

Mr. and Mrs. Froggatt were nice, as I recall, and they explained that we would all have jobs to do while we were there. I don't remember what mine were. I don't remember the bedrooms or anything else about the house—perhaps because I was there just a short time. I was told that on Friday, I would be taken to my new home in a different city, and one that was not in Chippewa County but in Saint Croix. All I could do was wait and wonder.

Friday, just after lunch, my fairy godmother arrived. She even looked like one. She was prim, proper, and very professional. She wore glasses and was a little plump—with sensible hair, makeup, clothes and shoes, and a friendly, patient attitude. I learned that her name was Miss Lillian Hartfiel, and she would now be my social worker. *Thank heaven!* I thought. No more Mrs. W. with her short black hair that matched her disposition.

Miss Hartfiel told me that I was going to Glenwood City, a town about the same size as Cadott, to live with a family there with parents who were looking for a girl my age to help with their seven children and who were willing to provide a safe home for me. Luckily for me, they were Catholic. My mother went back to the church of her family after my dad disappeared (because he would never let her go to church), and we also became members of that religion. According to the guidelines for foster kids, I was told a child had to be placed with a family, if possible, that was of the same religion.

Three o'clock, front door, three-year-old grinning face and smiling eyes: curly-haired Franny at the door, looking through the beveled glass window. What a welcome! Mary—young, pretty, friendly—was also welcoming me. Georgie and Ray-Ray, up in their cribs. Now home from school, blonde, delicate Michelle, peering over her little pink glasses. Older brothers, Andre` and Rollie, studying me with quiet interest and curiosity. Louis, off to the side, skeptical of this unfamiliar person in their midst. *Where was Zoa who was usually here?* they must have thought. Richard, the father, who was an attorney, was the last to arrive. Gregarious and outgoing, with a ready laugh that radiated throughout his body, he greeted me. We chatted a bit, including what we would have for supper. Because it was a Friday and no meat for Catholics, he said, "You know how to make pancakes, don't you?" And then came the trademark hearty laugh all the way to his feet.

Ruby, Ken, and Ed would be taken the following week to a farm near Turtle Lake, and we learned later that they were used as farmhands, even though they were just fourteen, twelve, and eight years old. Thankfully, that did not last long, and they were taken to other homes. Ed went to live in Hudson with the Rileys, who legally changed his name to theirs. Ruby was sent to live with Chester and Helen Guingrich, who farmed in rural Dallas, near Chetek. Ken was sent to the first of many foster homes. He told me when we were grown that he learned all he could from each family, then deliberately got himself in trouble so that he could be moved again to learn more from someone else. He ended up staying the longest with a man who lived in the Ellsworth area, and Ken liked him very much.

Marlene and Jim, both younger than I by six and ten years, would be taken out of our home at a later time to live with an older couple, the Ettens, who lived in Boyd. Gladie was married by this time, Louis had dropped out of school and joined the army, and Irene had been taken out of the house and placed in a foster home between Gilman and Holcombe earlier, which was the impetus for my move and that of my other siblings.

CRAZY GEORGE

One of the first memories I have of someone trying to take advantage of me was our sister Gladie's first husband, Crazy George. We always called him that because his eyes, even though physically beautiful, had that evil look that went all the way through him, and we never trusted him. We could tell that he intended to do us harm. He would always say that our sister needed us to help babysit or to help with housework. We knew better. Riding back with him, after babysitting, in his car or old junk truck as he sped around Stifter's Curve, he always tried to get at us, so we knew that we needed to be wary and on watch.

He was reckless, drove without regard for others, and one time rolled his vehicle, but survived. Ruby told me that one time, he tried to bother her while driving her home, and he stopped the vehicle. Luckily for her, another vehicle came by, and she told him, "You get this car going, or I'm gonna scream." He did, and she was safe that time.

Thank goodness for Old Bill Grewe's (said Gravy's) alfalfa field to the south of where we lived. Easily four feet tall and in full bloom now, the dense forest of green and lavender provided a good shelter for us. We'd done this before—this hiding out.

Sometimes, when we hid in the alfalfa, we had Ken with us, and instead of running in fear, we sneaked away quietly, an unopened package of graham crackers in tow. We had a little section matted down as our secret hideaway, where we pulled blossoms apart and sucked the nectar out of the ends of the clusters while looking up at the clouds in the sky. We imagined no troubles and dreamed the dreams of other times or places.

The heat was oppressive, and the annoying flies and mosquitoes, always an irritating nuisance in the day and early evening, had settled down in the dark. Ruby and I, on our narrow cot and in our customary position like spoons in a drawer, had nearly drifted off to sleep when we realized there were intruders. Through my presleep haze, I realized it was just my brother Louis—but along with him, Crazy George. Trouble ahead, we could tell. I might have known he'd come for me sometime when I wasn't able to flee to the alfalfa hideaway.

I was young then, in my early teens, probably fourteen going on fifteen, short and slender—no match for him—strong and wily, but more than that, resolved to try to have his way with me and to own me.

Bev on rounded concrete steps leading into basement.

Lifted out of my bed, I loudly protested and tried to get away, but he was resolute. Working with old junk metal and on farms had helped him get as physically strong as he was mentally determined.

There was some small consolation that my brother was present, but that was to be short-lived. Restricted in the car somehow (my memory has blocked that out), Crazy George drove out in the country somewhere west of town, and soon he sent Louis away. My brother, a gentle soul and learning disabled, I believe, now that I am familiar with that disability or brain damaged from having been thrown against the concrete wall more than once, complied. Crazy George was extremely controlling, and in fact, now he would be called a control freak. So Louis did as he was told and walked down the road and away from protecting me.

For the remainder of the night, I fought that stinking jerk off. I'd be darned if I'd submit, even if it cost me my life. His tobacco breath, sweat, and body odor were as offensive as his actions. Looking back later, I wondered why he didn't just strangle me or knock me out. It must have been that he thought he could succeed, and if not now, then later. I think that, because I had strong biceps from all the hard work I had done (like picking rocks off farmers' fields, carrying buckets of maple sap, mixing and hauling concrete, doing construction work, cutting wood, and gardening), I was able to keep him from overpowering me. We kids often played with each other by flexing our muscles to show our strength. The most strength though, I believe, was that which was provided to me by divine intervention that night. Crazy George must have considered me the ultimate challenge. He didn't know that he was dealing with a feisty survivor with a stubborn Bohemian and German temperament who had plans of her own for her future, and they certainly didn't include him.

When he finally had to give up and accept defeat in the early morning hours, he drove to his and my sister's house. I told her what happened, and she checked me to inspect for damage.

Thank goodness I was able to thwart his plans. Crazy George did not succeed with me because I wasn't interested in being a victim. I would not agree to submit because I instinctively knew that I would not get anything out of that. All my life, I had vowed to myself that I was not going to live the way my mother had to. I wanted a good, productive, upright life for myself, not one of poverty and degradation, and if I died in my efforts, so be it. I couldn't, and wouldn't, give in and submit. If I lost my virtue against my will, I would lose my soul as well; and it would be an arduous undertaking and a long journey to reclaim it. When I would love someone, and whom I would become intimate with, would be my decision, not someone else's.

One of my sisters did not have my good luck and same fortunate outcome in escaping this evil devil. It was during the wintertime, late

'55 or early '56, when her life went haywire, tripped up trying to get away by the very railroad tracks she had walked all her life. Crazy George was bringing her back from babysitting, stopped the vehicle and she took off running down the tracks. She tripped on one of the ties and fell. He caught her by the hair, and dragged her over the ties, spoiling her plans of escape.

I was doing homework at the kitchen table located below the bigger window to the north of the "garage" where we were living at the time. The track of headlights on the wall announced that someone had driven into the yard. I stood up on the chair to look out and saw Crazy George's truck that he used to haul scrap metal to Phillips' junkyard in Eau Claire. My sister brought home from babysitting, it appeared.

But I was wrong. Instead of a peaceful time of caring for small children, she had been violated in the worst possible way. Crying, disheveled, and distraught, she entered the house. My mother knew immediately what had happened and took her at once to Dr. Haines. He confirmed what had happened, and my sister was taken straight to jail. Yes, I said jail. Not that she had done anything wrong, of course, but for her own protection. Dr. Haines reported the crime to the police, and she was taken to jail by the sheriff to be safe.

My sister never came home again. She had to stay in jail for quite a long time until the trial was over and Crazy George was sent to prison in Waupun. This sister is now in her seventies, and sadly, she has never known a day of romantic love in her life and still lives in poverty and under control of others.

During Crazy George's trial, his lawyer tried to coerce us younger kids to lie on the witness stand for his benefit by saying that he had a different vehicle than he actually had. I remember internally struggling with this as I knew that what he was asking us to say was wrong, and I think that the judge realized this and did not make us stay very long on the witness stand. I don't know why that lawyer thought that we could testify on Crazy George's behalf, encouraging us to lie.

Crazy George had originally come from one of the Native American tribes in Upper Michigan, placed on a small farm with the Douvilles, French-speaking, kind people who lived southwest of Cadott. Oliver and Philomena were old by then, and their son Clifford still lived with them. The Douvilles were friends of the Shaffers, people whom Gladie babysat and shoveled manure for. Mr. Douville employed Crazy George's uncle who was instrumental in bringing him to the Cadott area. Gladie was already working for the Douvilles on their dairy farm in response to an ad in the newspaper.

Crazy George was on parole when my sister Gladie met him in the summer of 1954, after her high school graduation. He went by various surnames, and we never learned for sure what trouble he had been in when he lived in Michigan. We did learn of a car accident he had been in there, so perhaps he was on parole because of that. I wouldn't be surprised, however, if he was in legal trouble because of crimes against women. Gladie told me that she didn't love him, but married him on August 24, 1954, because she was "looking for a home." She also was pregnant at that time. They drove over to Stillwater, Minnesota, because there wasn't a waiting period there, and they could be married right away.

They lived with the Douvilles for a while, and when I was with them there, it was determined that I would sleep in the same bed as they did. That was ludicrous, now that I look back on that time. Gladie was on one side of the bed, and Crazy George took the middle, which I didn't like as he kept trying to fondle me when all I wanted to do was sleep. I finally went into the living room to sleep on the couch to get away from him when I realized his intentions. Irene told me that she used to hide under the bed to get away from him, and he kept reaching under there, swearing at her because he couldn't locate her.

The rest of us wished that Gladie had married Cletus, the nice young man she had dated in the spring and early summer of that year. Cletus would drive up on his beautiful early-1950s Harley Davidson. Painted robin's-egg blue and appointed in white leather, with fringe that flowed from the handle grips, it was a magnificent beauty—about as striking as its owner. Cletus was a fine specimen of a man—tall, blond, extremely handsome, and a gentleman through and through, but I think he had a wild streak too. My brother Ken told me that when Cletus came right up close to the door and revved the controls, that "scared the hell" out of him.

Cletus holds a special place in my memories because it was he who gave me my first real kiss, even though I was just a young teenager, a deep, toe-curling kiss that I learned some years later was known as a French kiss. Scandalous, no doubt, in those days, but exciting nonetheless to a young girl just awakening, and nowadays considered run-of-the-mill, at least in the movies. Sadly, we learned sometime later, Cletus lost his life while still a young man in an accident on a bridge between Cadott and Boyd, his hometown. I think he mangled the motorcycle too.

Gladie and our mother had some kind of disagreement, and she told me that our mother planned to throw her out, though one of my other sisters told me that she ran away. This sounds cold and harsh; however, that was not uncommon back then. Young people, especially those from large families, were ousted from the nest as soon as they turned eighteen or graduated from high school. My husband told me that he and his brothers were strongly encouraged to join the service and get going on their own as soon as possible.

My sister Irene told me that she dropped out of school and was coerced into a loveless marriage at an early age by her husband's family because they were tired of having him around and he ate them out of house and home. They pawned him off on Irene, and she allowed that. Relatives on his side planned the details of the wedding, and Irene was stuck in that situation for about forty years, mainly as a maid and caregiver, a consequence of her earlier traumatic experience. She is still waiting to meet a nice man, still waiting to live.

Upon reviewing one of my diaries that I kept for many years, I found my brief comment on May 21, 1959, a day before my high school graduation, about Crazy George getting out of prison. What a travesty—him serving only about two years for ruining a young girl's life.

Crazy George continued to try to get at me, and he continued to write to me while he was there in Waupun, though I never knew it. Mary, my foster mother, thank goodness, never gave the letters to me or told me about them until I was a grown woman and mother. He never gave up until he did himself in in his car with carbon monoxide poisoning. Irene, Ruby, and I did not shed any tears for him. We were relieved he was gone, out of our existence. We were still together in family spirit, moving ahead in our lives as we did during our early days in poverty, living our life of survival.

RUBY'S HARROWING EXPERIENCE

As I was gathering information for my writing, I spoke with my sister Ruby about our shared experiences. One experience she told me about, however, was solely hers. She too was determined to not be a victim when she was a young lady.

She was about to graduate from Chetek High School in 1961 and had decided to join the air force with a classmate in the Buddy Program. They had gone into Minneapolis for their physicals and had taken the bus back to Eau Claire for a connecting bus to Chetek. Somehow, they missed the bus. Ruby wanted to call Chester and Helen to come for them.

"Not to worry," a well-dressed, handsome man from Elk Mound said and offered them a ride. Ruby, always wary, did not want to accept the ride, but her classmate, "Stupid Sissy with the big breasts," willingly climbed into the middle of the bench seat of the blue 1953 car with the hooded headlights, big back fender skirts, and a long white chiffon scarf draped over the rearview mirror. Young ladies wore such scarves in the '50s and '60s to wrap their hairdos gently but securely with the ends hanging down their backs or tied gently at the back of the neck, when riding in cars, especially convertibles.

Before long, it was clear that they were going the wrong way, away from Eau Claire and not in the direction of Chetek. "Oh, yeah, I know a shortcut," he said and pretended to be stuck in the sand. "I want to do something to you girls. I want to eat you," he said.

Being young and naive and well before the days that oral sex was even discussed or became more accepted and mainstream, Ruby told me she did not understand at first.

Soon, however, she realized that they were in grave danger. Taking a gun out from under the seat and knocking it on the steering wheel, he let them know that he was in charge. Ruby jabbed and poked Sissy in the side, urging her to get out of the car with her. Grabbing their luggage and running down the road toward Elk Mound, the man followed along the road, calling out, "I'll find you girls."

"Lie down!" Ruby told Sissy as they hid in the viaduct. Over the railroad tracks they scrambled, water all over. Falling on downed trees that were all over the road because of a widening project, they ran and stumbled. Ruby lost her high-heeled shoe, ripped her nylon stockings, and fell over an embankment and culvert, scraping her knees and hands on the gravel. Tree stumps gouged into her chest, leaving black-and-blue marks for a long time. Either from the stress or an injury, her period came early, adding to her distress and problems.

They walked for a long distance on the tracks before finally coming to a farmhouse. The farmer who answered the door was shocked, seeing them disheveled and frightened. When he saw Ruby with blood running down her legs, he thought that they had been in an accident. He called his wife to help them clean up and to tell them what had happened. He helped them contact the police to report the incident. The police found the car, just as Ruby had described it, parked in front of a bar. Those long days as a kid playing identifying and counting cars with us siblings paid off in spades.

The police brought the man out for Ruby and Sissy to identify, and he was to appear in court the next day. They did not press charges as the man's wife was in the hospital, having delivered her third baby. Another girl came forward and told the authorities that the man had started to get the scarf around her neck during a similar situation.

Ruby called Chester and Helen. The police made a county-to-county transfer, and Ruby and Sissy went home safely. When it came time for enlistment day, Ruby's "buddy" never showed up, so she went on alone. Just as well, for with a buddy like that, she was better off going on her own. Ruby ended up as a dental technologist and dental hygienist and worked in her profession for over fifty years.

We have often talked over the years about our fierce determination as young girls to not become victims. We never saw ourselves as victims even though we lived in poverty. We always hoped and dreamed of living a better life as grownups. Sometimes, our existence was idyllic, living as we did amid nature at the edge of town, but it was a harsh life overall. We lived off the land and were connected to it daily in our struggle to survive.

MY FAMILY

Early memories of my family began when I was about four years old and centered around family members and the house we lived in at that time. We lived just a block from busy Highway 29, a main road that was heavily traveled in the summertime by tourists who came to God's Country in the Wisconsin area often called Indianhead Country because that part of the state resembles the profile of a Native American (called Indians back then). The last of seven homes on Poplar Street at the southwest edge of our small village, we lived in an old T house next to farmers' fields of corn and alfalfa to the south and a pasture for cows to the east. My sister Ruby and I loved to push our baby brother Ken in an old black wicker baby buggy on the sagging porch at the west end of the house.

Also living on our gravel street was Mrs. Walton (a widow, I think), close to the highway on the west side. Her house always smelled of kerosene or fuel oil and that old familiar smell of age when we visited her. The Walduskys lived south of her. Art was the local constable, and sometimes we had to go there for his assistance. I don't ever remember seeing or talking with Mrs. Waldusky. The Freagons lived on that side also. They had a house full of boys, and I don't remember ever seeing either parent up close.

We were told not to bother our neighbors. One time though, my brother Ken told me, when we were grown, that he interfered one time over there. Mr. Freagon, Ken said, couldn't drink cow's milk and raised goats that he milked and kept staked in the back. Ken moved the stakes that tethered the goats so that they were in the garden and ruined some crops, especially the green beans. He loved playing jokes on others; however, that wasn't funny to the Freagons, I'm sure.

On our side of the street lived Mr. and Mrs. Lancette, close to the highway on the east side. We liked them and visited with them sometimes when we walked by. Mrs. Lancette would later become our sponsor for both baptism and confirmation.

Clinton Smith was south of them. We called him Old Klinker Smith. He used to set trip wires across his driveway to discourage us from crossing there. I recently learned from a relative that Klinker had a blacksmith shop at the east end of his property beyond his driveway, so perhaps that is why he did not want us taking that shortcut. He didn't want us to get hurt or to get into his things, I suppose. I remember tripping on that wire more than once as we hurried to school. Ken has told me that we used to sneak up to Klinker's house and peek into the windows and to knock the huge icicles off of his roof in the winter time. Klinker used to sharpen saws for everyone in the area, including for the saw mill in town; and he didn't want us kids getting into his things. He sharpened the big saw blades in his kitchen, clamped in a wooden vice. He sharpened one side, then turned the blade around to sharpen the other side. Sometimes, if a blade had been warped, he would hammer the blade with a special hammer on the table to straighten it out.

Ed and Marita Zaruba lived between Klinker and us. Our large garden to the north butted right up against their lot. The Zarubas had two children whom I babysat regularly when Marita worked in Chippewa Falls at the Northern Wisconsin Colony and Training School, a large facility for disabled people who were not funneled into the general populace back then. We rarely saw anyone with a disability when I was a child, though people who stuttered, had a limp, or suffered from seizures were made fun of and ridiculed. I never participated in any of the teasing of people with these challenges and felt sorry for them, and I don't remember that anyone else in my family did, either. Perhaps because we were taunted and teased often, too, we had more empathy than some people for those who had some kind of problem.

We lived in our corner of the village according to the seasons and the land. The seasons dictated our day-to-day lives, and we happily went along with them. The land also imparts characteristics of itself to those existing on it, and it gave our lives structure along with the seasons. As surely as the seasons change, people change too. The land, though, remains constant.

My mother understood the land from which she drew strength. Just as the land was formed by glaciers aeons ago, my mother was shaped and formed by stronger forces than she into fertile, rich production. She was tied to the land each day she walked on Earth. Her very life was intertwined and woven into the land by her hard work, sweat, and bleeding hands. Because she worked so hard and had so much to do, she sometimes seemed like a stranger to me. She could be distant and guarded as well as secretive, substantiating the reputation of the Scorpio sign she thought she had been born under. She never had any respite or private time; perhaps that is why she knitted in peace and quiet during the long winter nights.

My mother on the land she loved.

My mother was used by nearly everyone, subservient, put in her place before Women's Liberation came into existence. The very conception of each of us kids was most likely the result of her responding "Umm-hmm" to my dad's question, overheard by us in the confined spaces of the night, "Do you want me to make you another one?"

Women back then did not say no, and they did not realize that they had the right to reject sexual advances, especially if they were presented in a boorish, less-than-thoughtful manner. My mother was a strong woman, nevertheless, stoic in her responses to stress, upheaval, disputes, and mistreatments. My mother was slender and strong, with a figure and personality that was most attractive. She had shapely legs, lovely skin all her life, and a calm temperament most of the time. She listened well, said little, and could come back with a zinger when least expected.

Listening to my mother tell stories, sing songs, and highlight the olden days was a favorite activity of my eight siblings and me. The harsh, poverty-stricken conditions we knew were softened by her magical way with words and repetition, laying the groundwork for my eventual choice of profession. Her eighth-grade education, always a source of despair and frustration for her, did not prevent her from spinning tales of beauty and joy. Forgotten, for the moment, were the taunts of other children, the drunken fits of rage and beatings of my dad, and the grim reality of our existence. We would ask her again and again to tell us of the excitement of dancing at Rainbow Gardens as a young lady or to sing once again "Froggy Went A Courtin'" or to play "button, button, who's got the button?" one more time as we all sat lined up or in a circle. All we knew at that time was through the ears and eyes of children; however, our mother helped us to realize that there was a better life than we lived and that education could be our ticket out of poverty. Her all-time favorite recommendation was, "Get a good education. It's something no one can ever take away from you."

My mother always thought, or had been told, that she was born November 3, 1915, two months prematurely, when no modern medical interventions were routine, to Bohemian parents in northwest Wisconsin on the farm they worked about three miles north of Cadott. My research, however, indicated that she was actually born on December 13, 1915, just one month premature. My mother's name, according to her birth certificate, was Marie Agnes rather than Mary Agnes; however, I never heard her called anything other than Mary.

CADOTT: "HALFWAY BETWEEN THE EQUATOR AND THE NORTH POLE"

Cadott is now a village of over 1,400 people; however, when I lived there, it was less than half that. There is a billboard north of town, and the official geological bench mark, at the forty-fifth parallel three miles north of Cadott on Highway 27 that proclaims that the town is "halfway between the equator and the North Pole." Perhaps that is why we so often enjoyed viewing the Northern Lights during long summer nights.

Cadott has a history of farming, logging, light manufacturing, and fur trading. The village was named for the son of a French fur trader, Jean Baptiste Cadotte. During the War of 1812, he served with the British and functioned as an interpreter for the French. After the war, he was employed by the American Fur Company, which sent him all over the wild area of the Upper Mississippi. About the year 1838, Cadotte desired to settle for a while. He chose a site about three quarters of a mile southwest of the village and built a log cabin. I wonder if perhaps this was the log cabin that I was born in, as it would have been about that distance out of town and was old when my parents lived there.

Cadotte remained in the area for three winters and then left for Canada with no intentions of returning. Fur traders and settlers came to know this place as Cadotte Falls. A dam was built on the river near the falls, a tannery was started on the north side of the river, and these activities brought more settlers, homes, and stores.

Main Street

One store on the east side of Main Street was owned first by my paternal grandmother's parents, then by my dad's mother. She sold "essential groceries" to farmers for a number of years. My aunt Laura Wiseley, my dad's sister, ran it for a while, and my dad worked there for a time also, but he wasn't too reliable or dependable as a worker because he liked drinking better than working. Because he had access to the store—that must be why, in the late '40s or very early '50s, we helped my dad tear the place apart, salvaging the usable wood that he intended to use to build the house on the foundation of the basement my mother and siblings had dug. The white ceiling was that beautiful old embossed tin; however, as I recall, we did not salvage that. I understand that those embossed pieces of metal are quite valuable now. The dust was heavy in certain areas of the destruction, and the smell was that old, dry, dusty smell often present in attics that dries out one's nostrils. We got the boards home somehow, and there they remained, piled up against the side of the garage and never reused. They were destroyed, I presume, by vandals when they burned down the building many years later that had been my last childhood home.

MARTINEK FAMILY

My mother took us regularly to visit her parents on their farm she had grown up on. We always walked to Grandpa and Grandma Martinek's farm north of town to visit, all of us holding hands in a long chain, lest one of us get onto busy Highway 27 and get hurt. To the many tourists who used the highway in the busy summer months to go to cabins and resorts north of us, we must have looked like a flock of ducklings following their mother.

I vaguely remember Grandpa Martinek (William Albert), especially his handsome face, tan skin from working outside all the time, and his black hair. He was mellow and soft-spoken and was very good to us kids. Grandpa had come to Cadott, where many Bohemian and other European people settled, from Cooperstown Corners, near Manitowoc, a larger city in the southeastern part of Wisconsin. Census records of 1880 indicate that, in addition to Mathias and Antonia (my great-grandparents), five children lived with them in their home in Cooperstown, in the county of Manitowoc: John, aged nine; Elizabeth, aged eight; William, aged five (my grandfather); Wenzel, aged three; and Emil, aged one and one-half.

Information found in the 1900 census indicated that my great-grandfather, Mathias Martinek, was born in April 1848 in Bohemia. He came to the United States in 1860, was naturalized, was a farmer, and owned land and had a mortgage on it in 1900. His wife, Antonia Wesley, was born in May 1852 and came to the United States in 1870.

Three children lived with Mathias and Antonia in 1900. My Grandpa William (often called Willy, even into adulthood) had been documented in records with three different years of birth. The 1900 census states that he was born in May 1878, was twenty-two years old at that time, had been born in Wisconsin, and was a farm laborer. Mary, born in October 1884, was fifteen years old. Joseph, born in April 1888, was twelve years at the time and was at school. It appears that Mary and Joseph would have been born after the first five children of Mathias and Antonia documented in the census records of 1880. In addition, I remember my mother talking about her Uncle Joe, the father of her cousin, Marie, who worked at Marshall Field's in Chicago and sent us lovely clothing she no longer wore.

I didn't know for many years that Grandpa Martinek was blind in one eye due to a tragic incident. There are two versions of what happened. The first and the only one I ever heard was told to me by my mother. A conversation with my Aunt Laura in June of 2006 was different, so I am including both. My mother's version was as follows: While haying one summer, the horses Grandpa was handling ran into a hornets' nest, causing them to run wild and straight into a thorn apple tree. One of the thorns poked Grandpa in the eye, and when he saw the old doctor who served the townspeople (who was said to be drunk at the time), Grandpa was told to go home and was assured that his eye would be OK. It wasn't, however, for during the night, all the vitreous humor ran out, causing instant blindness and the need for a glass eye. My sister Irene told me that our mother told her that Grandpa was coming back from town, going north on Highway 27, when the hornets spooked the horses, causing him to be pushed into a thorn apple tree.

The version Aunt Laura told me is as follows: Grandpa was hurt in a logging accident (she didn't know where), and he spent a very long time in the hospital in Rhinelander. His jaw and nose were broken in addition to the damage inflicted upon his eye, according to Aunt Laura. Rhinelander is a long way from Cadott, so perhaps the accident (if that is indeed what happened) took place in that area. These may have been two separate incidents also.

My Grandpa Martinek did the haying, sometimes holding my sister Irene on one knee and me on the other, I've been told. He put Irene on the right side, with the "bad" eye, and me on his left knee, the side with the "good" eye because he needed to keep an eye on me. Irene told me that I didn't want to sit there and Grandpa would have to paddle me to make me behave. "And there won't be any cryin', either," he said to me, according to Irene, as he plopped me back down on his knee. I was probably afraid of the cutting blades of the hay cutter or of the rakes of the hay rake.

Gladie remembered sitting on Grandpa's lap while they listened to the news at noon on his Setchell-Carlson battery powered radio. She wanted to know how such a thing could come across as it did and she asked Grandpa how the people got in that box.

Grandpa also took care of the few dairy cows that always smelled so sweet to me and provided milk that was rich and delicious, especially as he had some Jerseys, which are known for their rich butterfat content in the milk. My grandma churned butter from the rich cream, with our help occasionally, in her big wooden churn that she kept in her kitchen. She also participated in the meal preparations for the threshing bees throughout their farming community, tended the garden and the hens, and the myriad other things a farmwife does.

My Grandpa Martinek died in 1946 of stomach cancer and was buried in Brooklawn Cemetery in Cadott, along with an infant son, John, and his wife, my grandmother, who died in 1956 of a diabetic coma caused by a kidney disorder, glomerulonephritis. My sister Ruby was with Grandma at the time she became critically ill and found that to be an eye-opening experience.

My mother recalled that Antonia Wesley, her grandmother, came to the United States when she was twelve, married at sixteen, had her first child at the age of twenty-two, and spent her life as a midwife delivering babies. My Grandmother Martinek was also a midwife who delivered many babies in the area around Cadott, including several of my mother's. I wonder how she dealt with all that stress. Perhaps because she needed to focus on the delivery process and the lives of others, she couldn't be nervous herself during a delivery.

My Aunt Laura told me that before going to the Cadott area, both my grandmother and grandfather worked in the limestone quarry in the Manitowoc area, which means, "land of the good spirit" in the Native American language used in that area. The work there must have been hard and physically demanding but most likely considered a start to achieving "the American dream" that so many people came here to find.

RYKAL FAMILY

My maternal grandmother's family was also originally from the Manitowoc area. Grandma's parents were Andrew Rykal and Mary Pruha, both of whom had been born in Bohemia and married there. Andrew was born in 1864 and died in 1942. Antonia, nearly always called Toni, was born in 1861 and died in 1934. My mother recalled that her grandmother had been born on Christmas Day.

Andrew and Mary (Pruha) Rykal had four children: Frank and James, Christina, and my grandmother Anna Rykal.

Grandma (Anna Rykal) was born May 12, 1892, and died August 23, 1956. She always wore a dress and clunky shoes tied at the front. She had lovely long auburn hair, which she braided and coiled at the back into a tight bun or other shapes. Most likely it was she who inspired my lifelong love of long hair. Sometimes she wore her hair in the style I would later wear for my son's wedding in 1994, and my mother appreciated seeing that style again.

Grandma, I realized when I took courses in my field of speech pathology, would have periods of dysfluency when she was excited or upset. She had a sensitive, high-strung nature, just as my mother did. One of Grandma's male relatives, who was nicknamed Peanuts, also stuttered. My uncle Emil had some dysfluency, and my brother Ed does also.

Grandma always baked bread for us when we visited, which she carefully portioned out to us. She would butter half a slice that was still on the loaf, cut that off the loaf, and cut that in half again so we wouldn't waste any of it. It was so good. My mother made the same bread all the years of my childhood, nearly every day. Sometimes, Grandma served us hamburgers that she had prepared and stored in oil, with gravy on her homemade bread. She stored these hamburgers in big crocks in her root cellar that had a cool spring running through it. They were lucky to have had such natural refrigeration to submerge the crocks in.

My sister Irene and I had the task of gathering eggs from Grandma's chickens, filling our aprons, which Grandma showed us how to gather into a container like a basket with towels between the layers of eggs. The chickens would peck the backs of our hands as we reached under them to remove their eggs. No wonder. Who wouldn't resist thieves stealing the next generation? Sometimes, Grandma gave us a big mitten to reach under the hens to protect our hand. Irene told me that we never broke a single egg. Grandma showed us how to grab the chickens by the neck to keep them from pecking us. Grandma led the way down to her cool basement through the outside cellar door and took the eggs from us, again without breaking any. She would wash each egg, pack it carefully, and then take the crates to town in exchange for money. Some years, it was that money that bought us shoes for school.

We loved Grandma's lilac trees, whose lovely aroma wafted through the air in the late spring. We also loved her row of peonies, which lined her driveway, perfuming the early summer air and offering us a place to bury our noses and faces in their cool, satiny fragrance. We would play hide and seek under the plants, being careful not to damage or break down any of the peonies, for we wanted to be able to continue to enjoy their heavenly beauty. We stayed out of Grandma's poppy bed as she used that flower as medicine and used the seeds in cooking. My mother remembered Grandma scraping the sap out of the pods for the natural healing benefits of the poppy.

Grandma often spoke Bohemian when she didn't want us to know what the adults were talking about. She and my Aunt Anna spoke the language, and my mother understood it but did not speak it. Grandma had some lovely cut glassware in a special display case, and I didn't know then that Czech glass is prized all over the world. I just knew that we liked to look at it and admire the way light danced off the cut edges. My mother had always thought that she would have at least one piece of this beautiful glassware; however, after Grandma died, my mother did not get even one remembrance of her mother.

BOSINSKE FAMILY

In sharp contrast to my mother's family, I did not know my dad's family at all, and I never once saw any of them. I was able to find information that indicated that both of my paternal grandparents could read and write. We had been told when we were kids that my grandfather, William Bosinske, came to America as a stowaway on a ship along with a friend with the last name *Helinski* or *Helenski* or something similar. The changing of spelling of names was common in those days, so I do not know exact spellings. My grandfather's traveling companion settled "somewhere in the Fall Creek area" of Wisconsin, according to my mother, and I have no information beyond that; however, in my grandfather's obituary, there is information that he too lived in the Fall Creek area at one time.

The reason for the voyage as stowaways, we heard, was that one of the two young men had murdered someone back in "the old country," which was somewhere along the German-Poland border. We were told that the other man was the guilty person, but the other man's family probably said the same thing about my grandpa. The full truth is not known at this time and lies hidden in history. With nothing to document the murder, it may never even have happened but was just a story we were told. My grandpa was born "somewhere along the German-Poland border" according to my mother. As my dad spoke and sang in the German language, I am inclined to think that it was in Germany; however, with the lines between countries having been changed so much because of wars, it could have been in Poland. I located samples of my grandpa's handwriting, which is elegant and curvy, in perfect cursive typical of that time, so that makes me wonder if perhaps he came from a background that valued education and neat handwriting.

According to genealogical records of Ancestry.com, the 1910 census records showed that he came to America as William Bosinski in 1889. The date carved into Grandpa Bosinske's headstone indicated that he was born in 1867; however, I know that sometimes information on gravestones can contain errors. Information found on Ancestry.com indicated that there was a Wilh Bosinske, born about 1863, who left Bremen, Germany, on the *Wesar* and landed in Baltimore in April 1889. There is no information that I have found about the rest of his trip from Baltimore to Wisconsin, so perhaps this is the point at which he may have been a stowaway (if that story is true). He was not a naturalized citizen but had filed first papers so that he could own land. The land my grandpa owned is northwest of Cadott, and the barn, house, and pump house still stand. My grandpa and dad built the pump house and foundation of the barn, and my grandpa perhaps built the house too. Dates on the pump house and the house remain and are thus: on the pump house, the date inscribed in the concrete is 1923, and on the outside northeast wall of the foundation of the house in very neat cursive writing is the date June 17, 190—, with the last figure chipped off and missing, so it had to have been built between 1900 and 1909.

Grandpa did not file second papers. In addition to being a farmer, he was a stonemason as my father was. According to my mother, he had two brothers, Ted and Herman, and three sisters, Matilda, Martha, and one sister whose name my mother did not recall, although at one time she or someone who had information told me of a Bertha Repp who was a sister. An Alvina Middlestead is also listed in his obituary, so more work is needed to clarify exact details.

BAKER FAMILY

My dad's mother was Magdalena (Lena) Baker. The farmers' directory of Goetz Township lists her name as Leona; however, I never heard her referred to by that name. I have absolutely no memories of her as she would have been fairly old when I was small, and I don't remember our mother or dad ever taking us to her home. According to the obituary in one of the local papers, Grandma was born in the town of Goetz on January 2, 1874, and married in Chippewa Falls October 16, 1892. She died March 21, 1947, and was buried, along with Grandpa and other relatives, in the Union Cemetery, which is northwest of Cadott in the town of Goetz, on Highway O.

I do not have much knowledge or information of her background; however, my mother told me that she was as wide as she was short and could barely get through the doorway. My mother said that Grandma's family was "uppity," "snooty," and "had money." I don't think that my mother was ever at ease with my dad's family, and her descriptive words may indicate her own feelings of not fitting in with them. In addition, my mother told us that when Grandma got angry at her husband or kids, she would stalk away and down to the cellar, where she would stay for weeks at a time as she had provisions down there. My dad must have inherited her disgruntled disposition.

MRS. FRANK Buske, former teacher at the Baker school in the Town of Goetz, which is to become the home of the Cadott Country School Museum, submitted this picture of the school's class of 1905, and she plans to donate it as part of the museum's exhibit.

Though part of the picture is faded too badly to be reproducible, most of the students can be identified, as follows:

Top row, left to right: Lillian Felsner, Edith Bosinski, Meta Polzin, Ida Post, Annie Boettcher, Anne Gumz, Hugo Post; middle row: Alfred Polzin, Bertha Gumz, Irene Polzin, Martha Bosinski; front row: Albert Felsner, Emma Hunt, Paul Bosinski, Martha Hunt, Freda Post, and Lydia Bosinski.

Baker School students early 1900s

Grandma Bosinske's family, though, must have been somewhat important as the Baker School, a one-room schoolhouse relocated to the park in Cadott and later across the highway to the Cadott Area Historical Society, was named for her family. According to information obtained from the Cadott Area Historical Society and Museum,

"the Baker School was located on the NW corner of the Junction of Co. Trk X and Co. Trk O. It was named after the Ed Baker family, early settlers who lived near by. The land was leased from Jacob Zern in 1875. The schoolhouse was built by Charles Spaeth for $25. The first school board meeting was held July 5, 1887, with the following officers elected: A.B. Hamlin, Clerk; Ed Baker, Treasurer; August Priebe, Director. The first teacher was Mary Wall. The last teacher was Elsie Fuchs for the term 1960-1961. The School District # 5 consolidated into the Cadott School District # 7. The School was moved to Riverview Park in May 1962 by the Lions and

is staffed by the Woman's Club for viewing. It was the first
school museum in Chippewa County. In 1987 the Historical
Society sponsored the Baker County School Centennial at its
present location in Riverview Park" (now located across the
highway near the Cadott Area Historical Society).

My father had an uncle (Gust Baker) and another uncle (Ed Baker)
in addition to an aunt (Mary Malone Prirvee), who had three daughters
and two sons. Ed Baker was considered the primary immigrant and
entered the country through New Orleans. I have not been able to locate
information about the travels from New Orleans to Wisconsin.

In chronological order, my dad was sandwiched in the middle of his
five sisters. Edith was born in 1893, though my mother said that she was
born before my grandparents married, which was in 1882, according to
obituaries. Edith married Christ Heberg and had two sons, Clyde and
Merton. Martha was born in 1895 or 1896. She married Bill Lange
and died pregnant at the age of twenty-one due to complications of the
gallbladder. My dad came next, March 19, 1898. A sister, Lydia, born
March 1900, included in an early picture of students at the Baker School
but about whom I have not been able to learn more, died at a young
age, sometime after early school age. My father had a sister, Clara, born
March 1901. She married Adam Jenneman and had one son, Charles
Jenneman, who lived in the Altoona area. Another sister, Laura Wisely,
was born in 1902 and died of a stroke in 1977. Her husband, Emmett,
was born in 1903 and passed away in 1976. They had no children. They
were buried in Union Cemetery along with other family members.

My mother did not know for sure, and people often did not keep
track of exact birth dates in those days; however, it was believed that
my dad was born on March 19, 1897 or '98. I found draft records that
indicated that he was, indeed, born March 19, 1898. He registered for
the draft using the name Paul Louis Bosinske (Louis being the English
equivalent of Ludwig, the name he usually used as his middle name)
during World War I on September 12, 1918. His signature was quite
nice, considering he skipped out and played hooky most of his school
days. While his sisters were in school, he was hiding out in the woods.
Those records indicated that he was five feet six inches tall, had blue
eyes, and light-brown hair. He was working as a farm laborer for his
dad in RFD 1 (Rural Free Delivery), Cadott. Because the war ended

November 11, 1918, he did not serve in the military, and I never heard him ever talk about anything political or military.

My dad grew up on what is now 240th Street (north on Highway 27 to O, left on 240th, half a mile on the right). The original house, barn, and garage are still in existence, and the pump house my grandpa and dad built is still standing.

MY MOTHER:
THE LADY OF THE LAND

My mother, according to her birth certificate, was named Marie Agnes (though always called Mary), was actually born on December 13, 1915, one month prematurely following her sister Aunt Anna ("Annie" on her birth certificate), born May 23, 1912, and brother Uncle Emil, born December 17, 1913. My mother was lucky that the only lasting effect of her premature birth was a lifelong problem with her hearing ability. After my mother, came Aunt Laura, born June 12, 1918. Uncle Bill, born October 25, 1920, played a mean harmonica and the banjo, was loved by all of us kids, and died at a young age of leukemia on February 14, 1965. Uncle John was "stillborn" April 23, 1923. Milly Marie was born March 11, 1926. My mother was closest to her sister Laura, who was our favorite aunt. The young men of the area, we were told, sought the attention of both young ladies, especially when dancing.

The Rainbow Gardens was a dance hall, typical of those which were very prevalent in northwestern Wisconsin even as late as into the 1960s, about two miles east of where my mother lived. The dance hall had been built by my grandmother's cousin, Frank (Stub) Rykal in 1930, so it was during the heydays of that dance hall that my mother and her sister went there. The floor was maple, and there was a large furnace in the middle of the dance hall.

The December 2004 issue of the *Cadott Area Historical Society Newsletter* contains information about fourteen such dance halls in that area alone, most of which are still operating to provide the social joy of dancing and socializing. The newsletter states that the Rainbow Gardens was a very popular dance hall, holding many wedding and regular dances.

Roller-skating was a favorite activity on the dance floor, with skaters sharing a few pairs of skates or metal plates with rollers that attached to shoes with a key, similar to those that other children my age used and shared with those of us without them. May Day dances with long streamers woven around each other by the skaters and barn dances were also held. Aunt Laura told me that she and my mother used to serve hot dogs and drinks to the dancers from a small concessions area off to the back of the hall.

The hall is no longer standing; however, a tavern that serves food is still in operation there. The present owner, Pat Burich, who is a shirttail relative, told me that the dance hall had fallen into disrepair and was torn down in the summer of 1986 and did not burn down as some people thought. An article in one of the Cadott Historical Society's newsletters states that the Rainbow Gardens was torn down around 1975. At one time, the dance hall had been used to store heavy bags of fertilizer that caused the floor to collapse, damaging it beyond repair, Mr. Burich said.

My mother met my dad at Rainbow Gardens, even though he didn't dance. He also took my mother to shows in Stanley, a small town about thirteen miles east of Cadott, with an automobile borrowed from Earl, his friend, and my Aunt Laura's boyfriend, who became her husband. Aunt Laura told me that the car was a touring car and was quite nice. I don't think that my dad was very romantic in his courtship of my mother, though, as I never saw any true loving attention paid to her. Nevertheless, they were destined to become life partners, but my dad's first love was drinking and going on benders.

My mother married young at the age of twenty while my dad was already "old" at thirty-eight. They had known each other "for about a year," according to my mother. In a rural area such as Cadott, there weren't too many people who would qualify as potential mates. Weddings in those days were not the elaborate, overblown events of today. A shivaree (noisy banging on pots and pans and other irritating objects outside the marital window on the wedding night) was the big event, following the wedding dance. The dance would have been preceded by a raucous parade of a few cars dragging old beer cans and other noisy objects through the streets of the town.

My parents married in Menomonie, a larger town west of Cadott, on July 1, 1936, at the courthouse on "a beautiful day, with clear, blue sky with no clouds," according to my mother. There was a question at one time about the year, as my mother said it was 1935; however, my older sister found in the Dunn County records that it was in 1936, and my own research and the marriage certificate indicates the same. I think that my mother always said that the year was different because it was a shameful thing back then to have a child out of wedlock. It is interesting, however, that Gladie's birth certificate indicates that "yes" she was "legitimate". People often seemed to have trouble with the truth in the old days, and refused to talk about things, saying: "Oh! That's in the past; no need to talk about that. Forget about it." Not talking about things or forgetting about them, however, does not make them go away or change the truth about history. As Ghandi said: "The truth is still the truth." People shouldn't be afraid to be right or to speak their mind.

In addition to the wedding year discrepancy, there had been stories about my dad being in prison in 1935 for stealing batteries from the local Ford garage. My sister Gladie always thought that a different man was her real dad, someone tall, dark, and handsome and sporting a stylish mustache who visited our mother occasionally, arriving in a shiny big black car. Gladie would be sent to the spring with a Karo syrup pail to get some water, and she thought that was so she would not know what went on while she was gone. Perhaps that was true, or thinking that could have been her way to deal with the dreadful treatment she suffered for many years. A real father could never treat his child the way he treated her, she always thought.

The attendants at my parents' wedding were Charles Klass and Marie Goettl. The Goettl name would become famous in country-and-western circles decades later as being the location used for the Country Fest music festival each summer.

We saw my mother's simple but lovely wedding dress and shoes a number of times through the years, and we girls admired the unique shape of the heels of her shoes. Later, I would learn (as I became a shoe aficionado), they were the Louis XIV style, which came into fashion again decades later. Occasionally, we could convince our mother to draw a picture of a pair of heels, which she did quite well.

DWELLINGS AND BIRTHS

My parents lived in small, simple dwellings through the years we children came into the world, including the log cabin that I was born in. Aunt Laura told me that my parents lived with my dad's parents at first and that my mother did much of the hard work on the farm.

Their first home was about three miles north of Cadott, in the town of Goetz. They would live there for three years, and this was the house where Louis and Irene were born.

The Globensky Farm, again, out in the country north of the Frog Hop tavern about one and a half miles, was the next home for one year. It was here that Gladie remembered an impressive Native American Indian named Winslow White Eagle who came to the door to ask permission to take some of the white ash for their handmade items. Gladie, being a small child then, was impressed by the full regalia, including moccasins that went all the way to his knees and authentic feather headdress. She remembers the chief as being very handsome and polite. When he came for the ash, he sometimes, but not always, had women and children with him. They gave some of their handmade baskets to our mother, though I don't remember seeing any of them. As there were Native Americans living in this part of Wisconsin, I presume that is what he was. I learned when I was an adult that it was Winslow White Eagle who originated the idea for the Stand Rock Ceremonial that was popular for many years in the Wisconsin Dells.

Before I was born, my parents moved to the Lancor Place, a real log cabin that was across from St. Rose of Lima Cemetery and close to the railroad tracks about a mile west of town. This log cabin could well have been my place of death as well as birth as one time my sister Gladie was found by my mother dragging me up the steep steps in the basket I slept in to prevent a hobo from stealing me. No one was going to steal her baby. The rest of that year was spent here before the move early in the spring of '42, when the snow was still on the ground, into the southwest corner of the village of Cadott at the very end of Poplar Street.

My mother delivered most of us at home, with only her mother or Dr. Zenner in attendance. Everyone who lived in Cadott thought very highly of Dr. Zenner, including our family. Luckily, my mother had no complications with most of us, as so many of the young women have today. Gladys Marie (Gladie) was the firstborn, arriving on June 9, 1936, in my grandparents' home. My grandmother, I understand, was with my mother in the farmhouse for Gladie's arrival, as she was a midwife, as was her mother-in-law, Toni Martinek.

Louis Paul (Butchie or Butchie Boy) second to arrive, twenty months after Gladie, entered the world on February 28, 1938, with red hair and freckles, the spitting image of our Uncle Emil.

Irene Ann (Punkie) came into the world in the wintertime, December 2, 1939. She and I were just twenty months apart, and after second grade, we were always in the same grade at school. Irene had bad eyes all her life and curly hair when she was young.

My mother told me that when I, Beverly Mae (Queenie), arrived on August 10, 1941, it was such an easy birth that I "just slipped out." It was a Sunday morning "around six o' clock." Irene told me that our dad gave me that nickname because he thought that I looked just like a queen. Irene also told me that he favored me and didn't beat me as much as he beat her, Louis, and Gladie.

Ruby Ellen (Nubbins) followed me out of the womb on July 14, 1943. Still, however, my mother's confinements were only half over. Ruby would be the most slender of all of us girls, and second tallest.

Kenneth Ray (though my mother always said "Roy") (Squeekie) was born on June 29, 1945. My mother told us that she nearly died because of some poisoning (must have been toxemia) and that thanks to Dr. Zenner driving her personally to Saint Joseph's Hospital in Chippewa Falls thirteen miles away, she survived. Ruby and I loved Ken and enjoyed pushing him in the big black baby buggy on the front porch of the old *T* house we were living in then that my parents had purchased in 1942 on South Poplar Street.

I remember when my mother was expecting our sister, Marlene Marylin (Mouse or Mousie because she was so small and had dark hair).

My mother was determined to get the gardens planted before the baby came on May 18, 1947, at home, though I do not remember her birth. In those days, kids were taken elsewhere until things were over, so I suppose we kids were too, or we could have been asleep as Marlene was born around eleven at night. My mother told me that she had talked with a fortune-teller at the Northern Wisconsin District Fair one summer after Marlene's birth. This lady (probably a psychic Bohemian as my mother was) told my mother that she would have two more children, both boys.

I also remember my brother Edward Lawrence's (Eddie) birth very well. He was born on March 30, 1949, at Luther Hospital in Eau Claire. The reason I remember so well is that I became aware that my family was different from others and harbored some dark secrets; but as a kid could do nothing. Eddie came closest to death of any of us while just a kid in a gun accident in our house. That is another part of the story.

My mother's last pregnancy was with another son, James Lee (Jim or Jimmy), who was born August 28, 1951, at the hospital in Chippewa Falls. Sometimes we sisters dressed him up as a girl, and he was too young to protest. No one knows why my mother never had any more children, but there was talk that someone had "done something" so that she would be spared any more. Nine children were enough, someone must have decided, even though there were a number of families in the area with sixteen, eighteen, or nineteen children. There was no birth control at that time, and my mother was still a young woman (just thirty-five years old), so perhaps what we heard was true. My mother told us that the reason there were about two years between most of us was that she nursed all of us as long as possible, thereby preventing conception soon after a birth. I remember well my mother's last infant and how sore her breasts were when she weaned him. We kids had to walk to town to get some camphor to soothe her swollen glands and stop the tears of pain.

HOUSEHOLD EFFORTS

My mother worked extremely hard so that her family could survive. There was no time for lunch, or coffee, or volunteer activities. My mother was skilled at and persistent in being thrifty and eking out survival. She was a true "lady of the land." Every day was full of hard, backbreaking work. I remember many days when her chapped hands bled from all the work she had to do. She had to wash laundry, including all the diapers and her sanitary cloths (salt, sugar, or flour sacks folded into pads), by hand in galvanized tubs and a washboard and hang the items outside. She hung the laundry even in the dead of winter when the clothes became frozen representations of the people who fitted into them. Often, she brought the stiff items in to hang them inside to finish drying. There was no dryer for her but the sun and breezes.

My mother hard at work. In background: garage, chicken coop, and toilet.
The basement we lived in is to her right.
Big willow is where hogs were suspended during butchering.

The soap she used was often the homemade kind, made from beef tallow and pork fat and caustic lye in a big black kettle over a fire outside. This soap left a scummy residue on the clothes because of the iron-filled water of our well, and my mother did not like having to use it. She was always proud of hanging out very white, clean laundry when she had good laundry detergent. Ironing of the few dresses we had was accomplished with the old hand irons that were heated on the cookstove. There was a detachable handle that was used with the differently sized bottoms. Care had to be taken to assure that the bottoms weren't too hot; otherwise, items could be burned or scorched, and if not hot enough, they were ineffective on the wrinkles.

Soap-making day was a dangerous day, and we were severely warned to stay well away from the burning fumes and crystals of the lye. My mother had collected pork fat and beef tallow for many months that she heated in the big black iron kettle suspended above a fire of wood. After cooking, the mixture was poured out to harden and later cut into bars. With no fragrance added, this was not a pleasant soap to use; however, it was often the only soap we had, and we had to use it on our hair too. Young ladies today would turn up their noses at such a concoction.

When we girls were older, my sister Ruby and I loved to help with the laundry. Later, a wringer washing machine made the job easier. Ruby got her arm caught in the rollers one time, causing her arm and hand to be flattened for a while. It's a good thing that she was small and slender. We considered hanging the laundry a pleasure, squeezing every single piece into its place on one of the three lines my mother had strung to the south of the garage. To this day, one of my simple pleasures is hanging laundry, sheets especially, out to dry. No fabric softener can match the fresh fragrance of breeze-dried linens and garments.

Early 1950s. Back, L to R, Bev, Ruby, Irene.
Front, L to R, Marlene, Ken, Ed

We lived a life of poverty in every way; however, there were other families who did too. We knew of other families who had a drunk as the head of the household, a hardworking, barefoot, and pregnant mother, and a bunch of kids who arrived with regularity about every two years. Some of these men were my dad's drinking and moonshine-making buddies, so we knew them too as their still was to the south of our home in the field, hidden in a pile of rocks. Sometimes, Louis and Ken would go up there and sample the brew when the men weren't around. Three brothers from a large family, who were my dad's friends, made their own liquor regularly. One time they were found in the river, drunk as skunks and sick from having made and consumed alcohol that they filtered through an old car radiator. Amazing what some people do for their addictions.

PLUMBING AND POISONS

As is true in many poverty conditions, we had no plumbing, but had to haul water from the pump that was out in the yard. Bathroom duties were carried out in warm or tolerable weather in the outhouse or toilet, which was small, covered in gray asphalt shingles, with three differently sized holes and old catalogues for use as toilet paper. I remember that we girls always tried to get and hide, for our own use, the white or pale yellow index pages because they were softer than the colored, slick pages that we always tried to make the boys use. There were times that we were afraid to go into the toilet when the bull was right there at the fence, just a short distance away. So close, in fact, that we could hear and feel his hot breath.

Mother by basement cupola entrance.
Irene (R) and Bev (L) washing cucumbers by pump.

The smell in the toilet was awful, of course, and in the summertime, fly eggs hatched into white larvae with darker heads, which wriggled all over in the pit below. We would sprinkle lime in the pit though the holes to kill the maggots, but there was always a huge problem with flies when the weather was hot. This would call for a full-out attack against them with the old-time pump-action sprayer filled with fly spray, which we now know was DDT. We all cleared out after helping our mother close the few windows and cover all the dishes and food with cloths. Then, she would spray the entire place, including where we slept, with this poison several times a week, so it's no wonder that one of my siblings now has Parkinson's, another has ALS, some of us have heart and blood pressure problems, and most of us have battled cancer (me included, two times). We swept the dead flies up and aired out the place; however, much of the poison lingered, which we were exposed to and slept amid.

In addition to the fly spray poison, we were also exposed to the white-potato-bug dust, which we always had to sprinkle on the plants to kill those squiggly pink worms, the Colorado potato beetle. We had to control those; otherwise, we would not have potatoes the following winter, so we were vigilant and had to use that poison. We also exposed ourselves to unknown amounts of poison every time we went to investigate what we could find that was useable at the dump. One can only imagine all the pollutants at that time when there were no constraints against any substance and people threw into the trash any and all kinds of junk.

Having no electricity during most of my childhood, the kerosene that we burned in the old kerosene lamps for light also would have been full of toxins. I remember going to Dugal's filling station not far from our house to get kerosene on a regular basis. We filled the bases of the lamps with that stinking kerosene, which burned with a smoky residue called soot on the inside of the lamp chimneys and would also have filled our living areas. It's no wonder that most of us developed allergies or chemical and environmental sensitivities as we got older.

My mother canned, gardened, pumped and carried water (or carried it a long distance from a spring in the ground during the early years of her marriage). Many times in the winter we had to prime the pump with warm water in order to get it to bring water up through the frozen metal of the pump. The metal could be treacherous too as we attempted the proverbial foolish act of sticking our tongues on the handle to see what would happen. We learned pragmatic lessons early through actual experience. Carrying the pails of water built up our muscles, and we liked comparing our strong, firm biceps with each other.

PICNICS AND LEECHES

We would be taken on picnics often in the summertime by the family friend, Bill. We all rode in his old truck to places such as Bob Lake and Marsh-Miller Lake or for picking berries or apples. The apples we picked were the big yellow transparent variety that made excellent applesauce, apple butter, or jelly. Picnic items, such as fresh lemons for lemonade, Watkins or Jewel-Tea nectar (pre-Kool-Aid days), sugar and water, bologna with olives or liverwurst, bread, and cookies, were bought and looked forward to with great anticipation as we rode to the day's destination. A blanket was spread out in the meadow near the lake. We feasted, frolicked, and enjoyed being out in nature. These were happy times for us, and our mother had a little break from her drudgery.

When we were at the lakes, we nearly always had a problem with leeches that latched on to our bodies while we played in the water. After discovering them on us, we would jump around, squealing and screeching, trying to get them off, and as I recall, the only thing that worked was to put salt on them. We had heard that lit cigarettes would work too, but we never tried that. They always left small holes where their teeth had punctured our skin, sucking our blood. We knew firsthand what a bloodsucker was. Even though leeches are related to the earthworm, which we dug and handled all the time for fishing, we never got used to the leeches' stretchy, squiggly bodies that reminded us of cut slivers of liver sliding out of our grasp.

CHICKENS

My mother bought about one hundred small chicks each spring from the local feed store. She bought only white rocks and leghorns for laying and as meat chickens, although once in a while there would be a small bantam rooster in among them, which my mother didn't like because roosters meant trouble. Another source of trouble was when hawks, that my mother called chicken hawks, would swoop around, trying to capture one of them. We often had to go out and chase the hawks away. We had a pet chicken one time named Arabella who was quite tame. When they outlived their usefulness or got too old, my mother butchered the chickens, stretching out their necks on a stump before whacking each head off with one clean blow of the ax, leaving the unfortunate bird on the grass to flop around, thus demonstrating for us the figurative phrase "like a chicken with its head cut off."

Feathers from the chickens would be sorted and thoroughly cleaned before being made into feather beds and pillows to ward off the harsh cold of Wisconsin winters. Cleaning the chickens was always a disgusting, stinky job. The chickens were scalded in hot water and then their putrid feathers were plucked out, generally by us girls. The feathers often stuck to our fingers, and it was hard to shake them off. Any remaining pinfeathers and hairs were singed away with a burning newspaper. After this, the chickens were eviscerated (being careful not to cut the gallbladder, which would spoil the flesh), washed, and cut into pieces for the next meal.

Sometimes, a chicken that was still laying would be killed by mistake, which my mother considered unfortunate; however, this gave us kids a wonderful opportunity to view that process. We were fascinated by the various stages of development and sizes of eggs inside. Modern-day chicken does not taste anything like that free-range, but fenced in, chicken of long ago. I always was given the portion of the chicken that contained the ribs and the backbone along with the neck. I think that the reason for this was that I had the patience and the dexterity to get every last bit of meat off the bones, an economical solution to stretching out the food supply. Any old birds that had quit laying were used as stewing hens for soup or chicken and dumplings. My mother's dumplings were the best I've ever eaten. She made them nearly as big as a softball, and she cut them with a piece of white sewing thread, into big, round slices. She would place the dumpling on top of the thread, pull the ends of the thread up, cross the two ends into an *X,* switch the ends into opposite hands, and pull down on the ends, thus cutting the dumpling cleanly and neatly into slices, which a knife would not have done as it would have compressed and mashed together the warm, moist dumpling.

FOOD

My mother was a great cook despite her limited resources. Flavorings were limited to mainly salt and pepper, onions, lemon, dill, and sage. She used cinnamon, cloves, nutmeg, and allspice in her baking and limited amounts of ground ginger. Her lemon meringue, apple, rhubarb, berry, and chocolate pies were delicious, made the old-fashioned way with self-rendered lard for a flaky crust. She often used leftover bread dough to make a Bohemian pastry called kolache that she filled with cooked prunes. We loved these and considered them a special treat. She made boiled dinner often in the wintertime of either pork or beef with carrots, potatoes, cabbage, and onions, sometimes adding prunes that plumped up as a nice surprise. Soups and stews were made when she had meat, and she stretched out her meat supply as much as possible to have more meals from her supply.

One of our favorite meals in the wintertime was pork with kale that we harvested from out of the snow. That was the only fresh vegetable we had all winter as we never had salads with lettuce or spinach. We helped our mother peel and then grate potatoes for potato pancakes, thickened a bit by the starch that had settled at the bottom of the liquid that collected in the bowl. We loved feeling this smooth starch between our fingertips and often played with it. My mother followed the thrifty Bohemian custom of not wasting anything, which one of her sisters took to the extreme. Occasionally, our mother would can beef that we had been given. This had a rich, full flavor, and she fixed it with noodles or dumplings.

We kids all helped our mother with the canning and washing of the jars she needed and all learned how to cook at a young age, preparing such items as eggs, potatoes, and bacon-lettuce-tomato sandwiches with our own bacon and vegetables. Every fall, we threw potatoes directly into a bonfire, as we had no aluminum foil, and even though they were charred on the outside, inside, we thought they were just fine. While waiting for the potatoes to bake, we liked to smell the burning leaves and organic debris, the earthy, primitive odor of something going back to its creator.

Venison from deer that our dad had brought home and processed was always preboiled in baking-soda water to remove some of the wild taste before it was used. Sauerkraut was fixed for many meals as our mother had made several crocks of it in the fall with large heads of cabbage we had grown. She spent hours thinly cutting the heads into strands before packing them tightly into the crocks, salting in layers, pressing everything down with bricks or heavy stones on top of a glass plate. She always flavored this kraut with caraway seeds, a true Bohemian seasoning.

One of our favorite dishes was pork sausage cut into narrow widths then fried and browned. Water, salt, and pepper were added to the pan, and this meat broth was ladled atop the beans and potato mush she made by mashing potatoes and beans together. It was filling, nutritious, and was what we often ate when we went home at noon from school. The potatoes and beans had been planted, tended, and harvested by us. We kids had the tedious job of shucking all the dried beans then pouring them back and forth between containers on a windy day to get rid of all the chaff, demonstrating, once again, the meaning of yet another figurative statement. On more than one occasion during these bean shucking and cleaning sessions, one of my sisters used to stick beans up her nose, causing our mother to be worried about getting them out.

One year our dad brought some mutton home for us. It was the most foul-smelling odor that had ever entered my nostrils. The taste was even worse. Perhaps we thought that because we smelled that odor when we had to clean the extremely dirty fleeces before our dad spun them into wool that our mother knitted into mittens and stockings. To this day, the smell of meat from sheep, even baby lamb, is abhorrent to me, even though all my sons and my husband like that meat.

BUTCHERING THE HOGS

The month of November, when winter was settling in, was butchering month. The two hogs we had raised and slopped (fed) since the spring would be processed into our meat for the winter by my parents and a couple of my dad's friends. My dad would shoot each hog in the forehead, then quickly, in order not to lose any precious material, he would slit each throat and catch the blood in a container to be used in blood sausage. My sister Gladie told me that she had the job of constantly stirring the blood so that it wouldn't congeal before being made into blood sausage, which was always the first job done in processing the meat and by-products of the hogs.

The pigs were lifted into a large vat of scalding water, hoisted out with a chain-and-pulley contraption and tripod, and then placed on a slab of wood. Their stiff, bristly hairs were scraped off with tools made specifically for this purpose, round metal discs with wooden handles in the middle. The heads were cut off to be processed later into headcheese, a typical delicacy of people in this area of the country. The brains were removed, later to be sautéed into a delicate dish, which looked like a large, fluffy omelet. We had no problem eating this as that was preferable to going hungry and really was quite delicious. The feet of the pigs were pickled for use during the winter, the same kind as found in nearly all the taverns at that time in the Cadott area (in addition to pickled eggs in big glass jars). The fat was rendered, and the remaining bits that my mother called cracklings were salted a little and eaten as delicious, crunchy snacks.

The animals were strung up with ropes to hang from the large willow tree in the yard until they were chilled thoroughly. I don't remember any wild animals ever getting to the hanging carcasses. The hogs were cut into chunks and pieces, with the hams, hocks, and bacon sides being cured in brine before they were hung in the smokehouse with a tough string my mother called binder twine. This was called binder twine because it was used in binding bales of hay, originally in a piece of farm equipment called a binder.

Abandoned garage & smokehouse (late 70s/early 80s)

The smokehouse was a small building my dad had built, in addition to all the other buildings on the land. It had a dirt floor on which a smoldering hardwood bed of embers was kept going continually by us kids, taking turns, until many weeks later when the process was complete. It was our job to tend the coals, climbing into the smokehouse through the smaller door that faced to the south whereas the larger door that faced to the north was used to enter the smokehouse to hang up or take down the pieces of meat. We had to use the smaller door so that most of the smoke would remain in the smokehouse and not escape, as it would have through the larger door. We used applewood or other fruitwood if we had it as that provided the best flavor. We had to be careful not to breathe in the smoke or get any in our eyes, so we had to squint our eyes and hold our breath while in there, but we loved knowing that soon this wonderful meat would be ready to eat.

Occasionally, as there was no refrigeration, a small amount of mold would have grown on the smoked meat, mainly the hams, as I recall. My mother just scraped or cut this mold off, and we ate the balance, with no one ever getting sick. I have never tasted ham or bacon that is as good as this home-cured, smoked meat was. Maybe it was because we had helped to preserve it and had slopped the hogs all summer in anticipation of this.

Smaller bits of meat were ground in a sausage grinder turned by hand and then stuffed into the pigs' cleaned intestines into the best-tasting sausage I have ever eaten. My mother flavored the meat with only salt, pepper, and sage, which we liked very much. We children usually had the job of scraping carefully with a dull knife or the back of a knife along the entire length of the intestines, which had been soaked in salt water, to remove the residue inside them. They had to be clean before the meat could be pressed into them with the sausage stuffer. My mother would cook these sausages then slice and fry them for breakfast or lunch. The blood sausage was made as well, and great care was taken ahead of preparation to prevent the blood from curdling. I always thought as a kid that this was weird but learned as an adult that many cultures use blood in their diets. In addition, we all loved eating the round "coins" of blood sausage my mother cooked in her big old black skillet that she always used for all kinds of cooking, even making oatmeal in the mornings in it.

TRAPPING

During the winter and maybe other times of the year too, my dad trapped fur-bearing animals such as ermine (sometimes called weasel), beaver, and muskrat. He had many traps in all different sizes that he placed in strategic places to catch the animals. One time, our cat, Tiger, came home with part of a front paw cut off by one of the traps. My dad taught us how to skin the animals then scrape the extra fat and tissue off, being careful not to cut or tear the skin by the fur, as that would make them less valuable. We turned the skins inside out then fitted them on to narrow boards with rounded ends, and placed them close to the stove to dry out. In the summer, I remember stretching some of the furs out flat, then stretching them even further to make them fit on to the sharp tacks all around the board before placing them outside in the sunshine to dry, skin side out, fur inside. The pelts made a crackling sound when the skin had been totally dried out. These pelts stank, especially if any of the glands had been broken or cut, spilling the liquid onto the fur.

We learned how to skin rabbits that we had raised and then process their fur the same way as we did the wild animals. My mother made muffs that hung around our necks for us to use during the wintertime to keep our hands warm, and occasionally she made earmuffs or little caps too. We had to care for the rabbits and were always careful of the bucks because they could be mean, and we had to be diligent in keeping them separated and away from the does when it wasn't time for breeding.

I had a pet rabbit that I wrote a poem about when I was in third grade. I won a white ribbon and seventy-five cents as third prize in a county contest that it was entered in. I can't remember all the poem, but it began like this: "I have a little bunny that is cute as cute can be.

Every time I play with him, he always amuses me." I remember that my mother helped me to think of the word *amuses* as I was writing the poem. I was awarded a certificate and seventy-five cents for my efforts, and that was my first attempt at writing that wasn't part of schoolwork, although I think that Mrs. Liddell must have encouraged us to write for the contest.

Our teachers encouraged us to write often and well and to strive for uniqueness in creativity. When we were in Mr. Collins's room, in seventh and eighth grades, my best friend Jeanne and I wrote several plays and poems and performed puppet shows in our own school and others. We spent every third hour developing complex plots and characters, including dialogue, stage directions, settings, costumes, and other details. I often wish that I could read these works today, but I do not have copies of them. The entire Chippewa County area seemed to be a hotbed of creativity fueled by a love of language passed down from one generation to another and tempered by the daily grueling work of a life of survival.

THE BASEMENT

There were many other jobs my mother had to perform, but the hardest job of all, I think, was when she and my older siblings dug a full basement with a pickax, shovels, and a wheelbarrow. My mother told me that it took them four years to dig the basement, working whenever weather would permit or when she could fit it into all her other jobs. I can still envision her dressed in my dad's old overalls and denim work shirt, strong arms heavily veined, her hair in a kerchief, looking every bit like a slender Rosie the Riveter in the wartime posters. Heavy clay clods, which became impaled on the head of the pickax, had to be scraped off, scooped up, and hauled away to be added to the growing pile of dirt to the north of the excavation site. I remember helping with this job of hauling the clods away with the wheelbarrow.

We younger kids played at the edge of the emerging hole, exploring whatever we could find that was interesting. One time, we discovered a nest of mice, and I picked one up by its tail. It didn't like that, of course, so it turned around and bit me. Strange, I wasn't afraid of mice or snakes, but caterpillars were anathema to me, and I avoided them like the plague ever since my brother and older sisters chased me with them and stuck them down my shirt or dress. I would run, crying, to my mother and hide behind her. To this day, I can't stand them and have caterpillar phobia, even though I can appreciate their uniqueness in being able to metamorphose into something truly beautiful.

We liked to watch for the thin, shiny sheets of delicate beauty known as mica, which, though ethereal, is surprisingly heavy, embedded in the clumps of clay as if they were sheets of gold leaf. I sometimes felt trapped in my life of poverty like that mica was trapped in the ordinary clay, as we younger kids reveled in its luminescence, catching the ever-changing rainbows in glimpses. We peeled away the layers and wondered about our futures that lay ahead of us.

Concrete was poured for the footings of the basement walls, and my dad laid stones in mortar to make the walls, fitting them into the walls like a puzzle in a practical pattern according to the shapes of the stones. Examples of his and his dad's work still are evident in many farm buildings in Chippewa County. The basement was never to go beyond that level, like a living entity stunted and destined to never fully develop. The top of this structure was covered entirely with tar paper that was tacked down with strips of lath. There was nothing but dirt for the floor when we first lived down there. Eventually, my dad poured sections of the floor as he got to them, when he wasn't drunk or on a bender (a prolonged bout of drinking, usually to excess and often to the point of insensibility). I remember us kids mixing up batches of concrete in the old wheelbarrow, using the garden hoe as the instrument of mixing, learning masonry techniques early. This cold, damp project—which required hours of blood, sweat, and toil—was to be our home for the next few years before we moved into the "garage."

The basement was sectioned into spaces with no walls or dividers of any kind. The kitchen was in the southeast corner, with only a wood-burning cookstove like those old white Monarchs, a table with benches, and a few shelves for holding the spartan dishes. The root cellar was in the northwest, where potatoes were piled directly onto the cool dirt floor and wooden nail kegs held carrots, parsnips, turnips, and rutabagas buried in sand. We liked digging the vegetables out of the nail barrels when our mother needed them for cooking.

The fruit cellar in the northeast section contained shelves which held all the jars of pickles and fruits my mother had canned all summer. There were also crocks of her homemade sauerkraut made from the heads of cabbage we grew each year and dusted with bug dust to prevent the cabbage worms from eating them all.

Sleeping areas were at the north (along the northwest, near the root cellar), and another sleeping area for my parents under the steps that led into the basement from the south side. These steps led up to the *cupola* (a Bohemian word for small entrance area) to the outside. There were just a few small windows to allow light in or to permit our dad to peek in to check if we were doing what we were supposed to be doing while he was gone. I don't recall any refrigeration until after my dad disappeared, and my mother got a small, basic older refrigerator that she purchased on credit (and learned about the interest rate called carrying charges).

My mother's dishes were the tin or enameled dishes used in camping or by the military, kept on limited, handmade, rough shelving. She didn't have any beautiful serving dishes, crystal, or china of any kind. She did accumulate some of the small bowls, sauce dishes, cups and saucers that were given away free in the oatmeal boxes at that time. They were blue, pink, gold and light green decorated with pastoral scenes, rather like a toile print. She also got some vividly colored metal glasses and bowls that came with cottage cheese inside. These were delivered by the milkman along with glass bottles of rich milk, I remember, when I was a little older, probably after my dad was no longer with us.

Limited heat in the wintertime was provided by logs we chopped for an old-fashioned metal stove, which made a big burn on my butt one winter when I slipped out of Gladie's hands after my mother passed me to her after a bath. Gladie told me that she was sitting in an old chair that broke and caused her to fall and to drop me against the hot stove. She told me that the burn was at least four inches across and that the scab split and that pus came out of it. (I'm glad that I don't remember that.)

The slop pail, a five-gallon bucket that had to be emptied each morning, was used for nighttime toilet needs in the wintertime. I remember sometimes having the job of emptying this bucket, taking it out to the toilet to empty it there. The stacks of feces froze and rose to impressive heights during the winter because of the extreme cold, so Irene and I had to take a stick and knock them down to make room for more. I vowed to myself more than once that I would not live like this when I grew up. I always knew that there was a higher purpose in life, that I was put on Earth for a special reason, to be a beacon, an inspiration to others.

The cold dampness of this shelter settled in one's bones like the gray, dingy cement of the walls. No floor coverings were on any of the cement floor, and my mother had to wash the floor on her hands and knees. It's no wonder that she developed water on the knee at a later time.

My dad and Louis (note bare feet on concrete floor)

While living in the basement, I remembered my dad sitting there, spinning wool into yarn, with his pipe in his mouth and the ever-present beer nearby or in his hand. Sometimes, when he was gone, we would take his pipe and smoke it, being careful to put it back in the exact place and position we found it. My mother had to wash and clean the dirty wool, and we helped her sometimes to pull twigs and other debris out of the fleece before he spun it. I liked to watch this spinning process, being reminded of the beautiful miller's daughter and Rumpelstiltskin who spun straw into gold in the fairy tale. Many times, while he was spinning, I had to scratch my dad's head, which he ordered me to do. I did not like this job as he rarely changed his clothes, bathed, or washed his head, and had dandruff in the wintertime. I thought that this was better than the alternative, though, so I complied. How nice it would be, I thought, to rise above and be taken away from all this miserable destitution. No wonder I read fairytales every chance I could. In most of those, things got better or turned out o.k. in the end. I wanted the same good fortune myself.

One time when I was scratching my dad's head, he grabbed me on the right side of my chest, pinching and twisting extremely hard. With shocked horror, I couldn't believe that he had done that to me, and I worried that I would get cancer there from the damaged tissue that was sore for a long time. Every night when I said my prayers, I asked God to keep me from getting that dreaded disease. Many decades later, that was the side that first got precancerous cells, causing me to have to go through surgery, extensive radiation, and recovery. The problem cropped up on my other side seven years later, and I had to go through the same regimen all over again. Luckily, I did not have to endure chemotherapy, though, as so many women do. I could not have committed to that. Next time, if/when cancer comes calling again, (as a third course of radiation would not be recommended) I plan to do only the natural method, get out my bucket list, and consider myself lucky in having had a great life overall.

Our impoverishment maybe could have been avoided if my dad had not frittered away whatever money he earned at his job, as he was a skilled craftsman when he was sober. His friends often took advantage of him and helped him spend his money on booze, or he would get "rolled" (money stolen from him by someone unscrupulous). One time when he was drunk, those friends took red barn paint and painted his beard with it. They then took him to Leiser's Funeral Home in town, stretched him out in a coffin (that for some reason was outside where they could have access to it), and left him there inside it. When he awoke from his drunken stupor and, seeing his beard red with what he must have thought was his own blood and figuring out where he was, he was as mad as a hornet when he realized what his friends had done to him. He tried to remove the paint with turpentine, which did not work completely. It took a long time for that paint to wear off as he refused to cut his beard. Even in those days, men did drunken jokes on each other.

A different time when he was drunk again, he fell asleep on the train tracks east of the old pickle factory. Luckily for him, his friends found him and pulled him off before the train came through. Another time, he was found drunk in the ditch out in the country.

I wonder what my dad could have been if he had not been ruined by alcohol. Unfortunately for all of us, he was not one of those people who got mellow and sleepy when drinking. I often saw my mother bleeding and bruised with clumps of hair pulled out. On two separate occasions, Irene and I rescued our mother from a worse fate. At least one time, our mother sent us to get the local constable, who lived two doors down from us, for help. At that time, there was great tolerance for atrocious behavior that was fueled by alcohol. Not a very good way to grow up, except that such experiences can be the impetus for striving for a better life.

BEER AND PARTIES

For big drinking parties, held often in our house and in houses of friends of my dad too, a "pony" or a keg of beer would be brought to tap. We were interested in this process and watched while they tapped the big keg or smaller pony and then inserted the spigot to draw the beer into their glasses or containers. This beer was very tasty, and I could see why the men drank so much and so often. They just had no control as they were (most likely) alcoholics.

My dad sent Ruby and me to Emerson's tavern many times with a glass gallon jug with the finger grip to get him some beer, especially in the summertime. We walked right in, told them what we were there for (and they could see the jug), and we walked out with the beer, no questions asked. As we walked back home, we often took a little swig, which was delicious (especially as beer was real beer in those days, with a nice thick head of foam). There was no light beer masquerading as the real thing back then. The foam always lasted until all the beer was gone. Leinenkugel's or Walter's Pilsner Beer were the main brands available at that time, and many cases of Leinie's went through our house. After a big drinking party that my dad and his friends had, the next morning we kids would go into the case (or cases) and drink whatever remained at the bottom of the bottles when no one was looking. In addition to tasting the stale, flat beer, we always liked to look at the pretty Indian maiden's silhouette on each bottle and on the case and learned the slogans: "Made with Chippewa water from the Big Eddy Springs" or "Walter's: The Champagne of Bottle Beer." Later, we learned other slogans as well.

During these parties, there was always music and singing. My dad often danced a jig and taught us to dance it, too. I think that I could still remember and do that today if I had to. My dad played the violin, that he always called a fiddle, and sang in German (sometimes naughty songs), and others played instruments too. There were musicians on both sides of my family as the Rykals were also talented. My dad and his friends always were drinking or drunk whenever they were doing some work. One time, while cutting wood with a tractor and saw attachment, one of his friends had his fingers cut off on his right hand all the way down to the last knuckle. For these sawing marathons, we kids had the job of dragging felled or rotted trees out of the nearby woods, and in addition, we had to pile the cut wood into cords, being specific in how we stacked the wood, every other layer being perpendicular to the previous one. If we made a mistake, our dad would make us start over again and pay closer attention to precision so the wood wouldn't tumble down. We often came across nests of mice when we took wood off the piles to burn inside.

According to Mrs. McConville, my fifth and sixth-grade teacher, our dad was concerned about our safety. One year, for the Christmas program, we had to be out after dark. He told her that he would let us participate only if she could guarantee that we would get there and back safely. She agreed to that, came to pick us up, and brought us home after the program was over.

I have only one positive memory of my dad. When he learned that the Soo Line planned to eliminate passenger service between Cadott and Boyd, he took some of us on that last ride. He was not drunk, as I recall, and we enjoyed apple cider and a pleasant time with him. It was odd to be with him, actually enjoying being in his presence and not to have to worry about our safety.

Sometimes, he would bring home a big round cheddar cheese chunk (which was delicious), and he also raised bees so that we could have our own honey (also delicious). I remember, in addition, the times he bought (or was given) frozen flounder, which were shipped in large boxes with dry ice. We were amazed that both eyes were on one side of the fish's head, one of them having migrated during growth.

DISAPPEARANCE

My dad disappeared forever on November 8, 1953, at the age of fifty-five. He had been working north of town and staying with his farmer friend. His disappearance was written about in the area papers for quite some time. A posse was organized, bloodhounds were put to work, and groups of men and high school boys spent quite a bit of time trying to find him. They had no luck.

Organize Posse to Search for Paul Bosinske Missing Since Sunday

A searching party was organized and set out at ten o'clock this morning (Thursday) to comb the area northeast of Cadott in an effort to find Paul Bosinske, who has been missing since Sunday night. Bosinske disappeared from the James Muska farm near Crescent at that time and has been neither seen or heard from since.

The hunt for the 53-year-old man started Monday morning when he failed to appear in county court to answer to a criminal charge filed against him. The jury was on hand at nine o'clock, the time set for the trial, but upon Bosinske's failure to appear, was dismissed until two o'clock in the afternoon, while the search began. At two o'clock when the hunted man was not yet found, Judge Orrin H. Larrabee dismissed the jury members and postponed the trial until December 10, or until Bosinske has been picked up.

The missing man had been employed at the Muska farm, assisting in the mason work on a barn being built there, and also at the Alvin Woodford farm in the town of Goetz. During the past week, he was also employed on other farms in the vicinity and was in Cadott on both Saturday and Sunday. He returned to the Muska home Sunday evening and disappeared from there that night.

Woodford and Muska are both bondsmen for Bosinske, having posted $1,000 bond after his preliminary hearing in August. Since his disappearance they have carried out a search, assisted by friends and neighbors, and by Robert Jahnke of Cornell who flew over the wooded area in his private plane.

On Tuesday the searchers acquired the aid of Wallace Rudd of the Eau Claire City Police Force and his two blood hounds. The hounds followed a trail from the Muska house to the barn, and then to the road, following it westward about ten rods. It is believed that at that point, either Bosinske got into a car, or the scent was covered by a road grader which had passed through shortly before.

In this morning's search, the party of volunteers organized by Muska and Woodford and consisting of several men from the area northeast of here and a large number of local high school boys, is combing the entire area, including the towns of Arthur, Goetz, and Colburn as well as adjoining parts, devoting more time to the heavily wooded areas.

At the time of his disappearance, Bosinske was wearing a light blue shirt, blue denim work overalls, a cap and work shoes, but no jacket.

Continue Study of Skeleton

Eau Claire pathologists today continued study of remains of a human skeleton found in the woods near Jim Falls on Thursday.

Preliminary examination of the bones could shed little light on the identity of the skeleton, according to Sheriff H e r m a n Pederson.

Eau Claire Pathologist Dr. Lindquist made a preliminary examination of the remains yesterday. A further—and more detailed—study will be made today.

Meanwhile, a Chippewa county woman—whose husband disappeared several years ago—was also scheduled to view the shoes and other effects discovered near the remains of the skeleton.

Discovery was made by a hired hand on the Cloverbelt Farm about 1¼ miles northeast of Jim Falls shortly before noon on Thursday.

Local officials estimated the man had been dead for "several months, possibly for more than a year."

Chippewa County Undersheriff James Cardinal conducted the initial investigation. Sheriff Pederson was out of the county on other official business when discovery was made.

Jim Falls Bones Said to Be Those of Cadott Man

Positive identification of skeleton remains of a body discovered in the Jim Falls area last week have been made, according to Chippewa County Sheriff Herman Pederson today.

The skeleton remains have been identified as those of Paul Bosinski, rural Cadott. The man would have been about 62 years old had he lived to this time.

Identification was made by Bosinski's former wife, Mary. There was no doubt in her mind, Sheriff Pederson said.

Key to the identification was a belt, found hanging in a tree near where the bones were discovered by a farm hand last Thursday. Mrs. Bosinski told Sheriff Pederson that her late husband's belt had been too large and that he had punched an extra hole in the leather.

Hole Revealed

Close examination revealed the extra 'home-made' hole, according to the sheriff.

According to records in Pederson's office here, Bosinski had been arrested on a charge of incest and jailed here for a time. He had been released on $1,000

Turn to BONES, Page 4

Bones

(Continued from Page One)

bond but had never showed up in court on the trial date.

Sheriff Pederson said several rumors that the man had been seen in Minnesota and parts of Wisconsin had been reported. But Bosinski never returned home.

The sheriff told the Chippewa Herald-Telegram that the remains of the body had been at the spot on the Cloverbelt Farm, 1¼ miles northeast of Jim Falls, for a period of about six or seven years.

"The bones were chalk white and well dried," Pederson concluded.

After about six and a half years, remains that appeared to be his were found on the Cloverbelt Farm off Highway 178 in the town of Anson, near Jim Falls. The report stated: "Skeletal structure of human. Cause of death undetermined." My mother always thought that our dad was killed by someone, but had no hard evidence. My dad suffered from pleurisy every winter and a throat problem that my mother thought was cancer, so that may have been what he succumbed to. We will never know the full story of his ultimate demise. My mother viewed the remains, which included a portion of shirt fabric, and identified a belt found in a tree near the remains as being his. My dad was small, and he had punched an additional hole in the belt so it would fit him, and the belt that was found matched that description. I did not know any of this at the time but found out months later. His remains were buried May 13, 1960, in the potter's field section at the northeast edge of Forest Hill Cemetery in Chippewa Falls, though staff there could not tell me which site was his because they had no way of knowing. It was sad for one so gifted in many ways to come to such an end.

LIVING IN THE "GARAGE"

The "garage," meant to be only temporary until the house could be built on the basement foundation, was our next home. It was a simple, spartan, twelve-by-twenty-four-foot structure, with just two small windows and one larger one placed quite high in the wall. This living space was divided in half by a hanging bedspread or something similar that functioned as a curtain. At the west end was the bedroom in which we all slept, containing three beds for all of us with barely room to walk between them. Ruby and I slept on a narrow, cot-like bed with no room to turn over or lie on our backs. Because my dad had already disappeared by this time, my mother slept with Irene and Marlene on an old brass bed with a sagging mattress (but very white bed linens). The younger boys slept three to a bed. This was a problem as enuresis was ongoing. The cause, no doubt, being our poverty and cramped living conditions. Because there were no closets or dressers, clothing was kept in boxes under the beds. With moisture leaking through the mattress at times, the clothing got wet. There was a small ladder between the beds that led to the low attic space above. It was here that my mother kept sauerkraut in the big crock and the big sack of beans, in addition to some photos and other things not regularly used. It was hard to see up there because there were no windows. A flashlight or the kerosene lamp was used to shed a little light.

My mother sleeping in garage on white sheets she valued.
Note tight space between beds.

No privacy was allowed for my mother or any of the rest of us. As we had no bathroom, sometimes we girls would see our mother changing her sanitary cloths made of old flour, sugar, or salt sacks or torn strips of old bedsheets instead of pads she could not afford. The pads were attached to her underpants with two large pins in front and two in back, as she did not have any other method of wearing them. These pads were soaked, washed, and used again and again, so sometimes there were stains she could not get out. This bothered my mother, as she always liked things to be clean and stain-free. People often talked in euphemisms, so this time during a woman's cycle of menstruation, when "Gramma came to visit", was jokingly called "riding the cotton horse," or "having the rag on." My mother used those instances to tell us about the cycle of life in humans and to teach us how we would need to take care of our own needs when that time came in our lives.

The kitchen area contained the bare essentials, except for plumbing. The only heat was provided by the cookstove. We still had to use the old pump and outhouse as before. No modern conveniences for us, though our mother's friend, Bill, brought an older icebox that was kept at the northeast corner at the outside of the garage. My sister, Irene, remembered that our mother had a hole dug at the northeast side of the garage and submerged a bucket in it. Inside the bucket was where she kept things that needed to be cool. The bucket was covered with a tarp or blanket of some kind and sand for weight and coolness. There was an old couch at the west end of the kitchen area, a chrome table with some chairs to the north, a small refrigerator, stove, and rough shelving for dishes to the south and east. The only door in the structure was at the northeast corner, facing east. Upstairs was a low attic, unusable as living space. I remember my mother scrubbing the linoleum floor on her hands and knees every day. Later, this chore was gladly taken over by Ruby, the cleaner and decorator among us. Freshly picked wildflowers on the table often were a testament that beauty could hold its own among degradation.

Bathing continued to be done once a week, usually Saturday night, in the round old galvanized washtub used also for washing clothes, in the same order as always, from youngest to oldest, I remembered, in water that we heated on the stove. My brother Ken remembered that all of us girls bathed first, so his brothers and he got the dirtier water. In some families, the order was reversed, from older to younger. Every day, however, we had to take a sponge bath with a basin of warm water, soap, and a washcloth. When we began to brush our teeth, and having no sinks in the place, we went outside to the edge of the garden to rinse our mouths. I don't remember brushing our teeth until I was probably about eight or ten years old.

We didn't have any dental or medical attention until I was about twelve or thirteen years old, when we went on welfare, called Aid to Dependent Children (ADC), after my dad disappeared and my mother had no means of supporting us. This is when we got a social worker who monitored our mother's goings-on and our progress in the system. With some money for our mother to spend on groceries, we now knew the pleasures of eating citrus fruits, pineapple, tuna fish, mayonnaise and Miracle Whip, "boughten" cereal in boxes and bags, bananas that weren't stolen, and having enough to eat without being hungry. Bags of groceries would be all over the floor until everything could be put away.

MEDICAL CARE

Dr. Landry was the dentist in town, and we didn't like having to go to him. His hands stank of cigar smoke, and he wore big rings with ruby stones in them, which dug into our cheeks as he worked on our teeth. My sister Marlene told me about his sanitizing methods, which would raise some eyebrows nowadays, if her memory is accurate. According to her, he would wash the tools then put them on the window ledge to get sterilized by the sun. Perhaps he did not have an autoclave. Marlene must have gone to Dr. Landry longer than I did, as she lived close to Cadott throughout her high school years and would remember better than I, as I last went to him at the age of fifteen.

We never went to the doctor, as I recall. We had to take big round iodine tablets two times a week at school to avoid getting goiter because we lived in the part of the country where goiters were common and called the "goiter belt." We also took one teaspoon of cod-liver oil every day at home, especially in the wintertime. We used to hold our noses when swallowing to make the feat more palatable. When we had bad colds or bronchitis, our dad would make us take a concoction he made of turpentine and pine tar that looked like molasses and tasted awful, as one would imagine. With the petroleum-based turpentine, I wouldn't think that would even be safe to ingest. The first time I remember being tended to by a physician was when Dr. Haines came to see us when we lived in the garage because we kids all had bronchitis and sounded like a bunch of barking hounds. I remember being extremely shy when he examined me because I was just beginning to develop. It's a good thing that we had some medical attention at that time because ever since that time, I have had to be careful of lung infections and recurring bronchitis.

I did have to go to the hospital in Chippewa Falls when I was about ten or eleven. We had been in the gym at school, playing leapfrog, when my hands slipped out from under me just as my friend Ann hopped over, landing directly on my head. My nose was smashed into the floor, and I had a bloody nose and black eyes for a long time. I was taken to the hospital for X-rays because it was so bad. The only residual effect is a crooked nose on the left side and some snoring from that impact.

LIFE

We continued to live in abject poverty, with two big gardens, the chickens, two pigs, wild berries, and freshly caught fish to sustain us. Previously, during the war years of WW II, things were scarce so many staples were rationed. There were rationing stamps for coffee, sugar, postage stamps, tires, and gas. I remember that many times, when my mother's coffee supply was low, she would have to reuse the coffee grounds for her next pot of coffee. Perhaps this is why she and so many other people were used to drinking weak coffee that, to me, tasted like dishwater. In the late summer or early fall, we kids took big gunnysacks (burlap bags) to gather milkweed pods with the floss inside that was sent off to be used by the military in life vests or flying suits. We were sometimes dismissed from school to collect the pods. We found this job fun and felt as if we were contributing to the cause, although we got no money, as I recall, for doing this work. We also picked up empty pop bottles and junk metal along the highways and railroad tracks and sold the items for a little cash. The ragman collected rags routinely, and these items were recycled somehow. It is interesting that Wisconsinites were into reducing, reusing, and recycling long before it became popular, and I remembered signs along the road, interspersed with the famous Burma-Shave signs, that stated there would be a $250 fine for littering back in the early 1950s.

Holidays were not celebrated to any extent in our house because there was never any money for gifts or expenses. We never believed in Santa or the Easter Bunny or the tooth fairy because we knew we were basically good kids—and still nothing special occurred. Gladie told me that one year, her teacher Mrs. Sherman gave her the large tree that had decorated their room at school, which she proudly dragged home. The tree was chopped up and burned while Gladie cried, not understanding why she couldn't keep the tree. Irene never understood, either, why the glasses the school nurse got for her were broken or burned. The rest of us never could figure out why any toys or photographs that came into the house were thrown away or burned.

Occasionally, a neighbor would bring over a basket of fruit, or one of my dad's friends would give us some hard candy, and one year I remember that my mother roasted a goose as her effort to make things special for us. One time, my sister Irene and I were going up the steps by the *cupola* when we realized someone was coming. We crawled and hid under the tarp or blanket there, thinking he wouldn't see us. It was a friend of our dad who gave Irene a bag of hard Christmas candy, giving her instructions that she had to share it with the rest of us, which she did. My Aunt Milly often gave us new underpants, which we liked very much as they were always pretty pastel colors, sometimes embellished with a little lace or ribbon.

The best gift I got as a child was a bride doll from my fifth-grade teacher, Miss Freese. She knew that I wanted one of those, and when I questioned her many decades later, she told me that she had, indeed, made sure that she "drew" my name in the gift exchange, keeping my name separate from the rest. The doll, in its box with the clear, see-through front, was small, probably about a foot or less tall, with golden hair, dressed in a formal long white bridal gown that went out all around the doll to the box's edges with lace edging, and wearing a veil. I treasured that doll, loving it as if it were the most precious thing in the world. Miss Freese (later Mrs. McConville) told me decades later that I just would not stop talking about wanting that doll so that is why she got it for me. I also remembered that Miss Freese or her mother made my sister Irene a cake for her birthday one year that all of us shared and enjoyed in school. Sometimes, Miss Freese would come and get either Irene or me or both of us to help her and her mother clean house. I think it was the other way around, her helping us. She would make swedish rosettes with a mold of different iron shapes screwed into a handle, and after they were fried, she dipped them into powdered sugar.

We all loved where we grew up at the very end of South Poplar Street, which was at the southwestern-most part of Cadott. Dave Nelson had a field to the east of us, which penned in cows for shipment and, sometimes, along with them, huge bulls. Those big bulls were a nightmare for us as they were always trying to impregnate the cows, running and jumping after them with their extremely long red penises throbbing and ready for action—a very visual, graphic depiction of sex in the raw for young kids. One time, a big white bull got out, ran around, and climbed directly up on top of the basement. I don't remember what happened, as we went running into the basement to hide from him. Ken told me that he ran up onto the cupola to get away and that he remembered the bull being shot. We were afraid of them because often they would come directly up to the fence when we were slopping the hogs, picking currants, grapes, or rhubarb, or weeding the gardens. We were afraid to go into the toilet when they were around as they were so close we could hear their heavy breathing.

PLAYING AND DANGEROUS LIVING

The games we played as kids were directed by the seasons, and we were never bored. We always played outside in spite of the weather. In the wintertime, we made snow angels, played fox 'n' geese, built snow houses and tunnels, and walked on top of tall snowdrifts or banks, trying to not fall through. When there was a hardened crust on top of the snow, especially along the streets downtown, we pretended that we were wearing snowshoes, gliding along as if by magic. Many days, we went home with frostbitten fingers or toes, even though the mittens our mother knitted for us were thick. The effects of frostbite never really go away.

During the spring and summer, we renewed our skills in playing ball, jumping rope, playing jacks, and the games annie annie over, red rover, and hide 'n' seek. Playtime in the fall centered around the leaves and back-to-school activities.

We had large gardens on the north and east sides on the three lots my parents owned, and big fields and brush, which belonged to farmers, were to the south and southwest. We loved to walk in the tall grasses, floating our hands over the seed heads. We often selected the widest grass blades, stretched them out straight, and pinched them between our thumbs, then blew on them to produce a whistle. I have shared that technique with my sons and grandchildren, of producing a sound with a blade of nature. We loved to pick trilliums in the woods back then as that plant was not yet on the endangered-species list. A beautiful brook, graced in the early summer by cowslips and buttercups, fresh, dainty offerings to the new day, ran along the south edge of where we lived. Even though it belonged to someone else, we spent much time there learning about nature and reveling in the pure delight and joy of being kids in the summertime.

We loved playing kittenball, softball, and other games in the fields; however, there was no soccer back then. In addition, our days were not fully scheduled as the days of children are now with all the "necessary" sports and activities. We could play jacks or marbles, jump rope, or skip along—whatever we wanted to do. We had no TV or video games back then, so we were always involved in learning, cooperating, and gaining life skills. We were allowed to be kids, learning and exploring on our own and suffering the consequences if we got out-of-bounds or were too careless. We smoked what we called Indian tobacco that we picked when dried. We also salvaged partially smoked cigarettes from along the highways, making sure to cut or tear off any slobbered-on end because we didn't want to put any dirty disgusting end in our mouths. Hiding behind the garage, we learned how to smoke following Louis's tutelage that always backfired into gasping, hacking, coughing spells. "Yah, you just swallow," he told us, and naively, we tried that but it never worked. It's a wonder any of us smoked at all after those bungled lessons.

We were also expected to help with all the work that had to be done and were often farmed out for no pay or bartered goods (except for maple syrup) for our services. We had to pick rocks off farmers' fields and throw them onto wagons (a back-breaking job), gather maple sap to be cooked into syrup and candy, weed and harvest rutabagas to be sold, and pick, for our mother and our aunt Milly, those endless crops of "pickles" (cucumbers) to be sold to the pickle factory in town. Here, the cucumbers were put into a brine and allowed to ferment. Later, the canning process would be completed elsewhere.

Pickle Station located on southwest end of Cadott 1920

It was in one of the vats of brine that Louis nearly drowned one time and Ken, another. Ken told me that he was running along the planks on top and he slipped on the pigeon poop, causing him to slide into the vat. Friends threw him a rope, and he was able to get out. I remember helping Louis out by first finding then passing a long, strong board to him. These big wooden vats were not covered at all, so anything or anyone could fall in. In addition, the pickle factory was old and rickety, a dangerous place to play around. We went there often during the latter part of the summer when we took all the cucumbers we raised and picked early in the morning at least every other day, sometimes daily, when the weather was conducive to those heat-loving plants. We had to wash all the cucumbers out by the pump before taking them in gunnysacks to be sorted, graded, and then sent on to the vats of brine. There was a big conveyor belt that all the cucumbers were placed on then shook and moved along. The small cucumbers that fell through first were the most valuable, then on up the line, from most value to least or no value at all. Those big old fat ones were the ones we took home and used in cucumber salads.

One escapade that I remember very well was when Ruby, Kenny, Louis, Irene, and I knocked all the oat shocks down in one of the farmer's fields to the west of town. I have no idea why we did that; just being mischievous, I suppose. Because Louis was with us, I would guess that it was his idea as he was always getting in trouble. We left the oats all tossed around and went home as if nothing had happened. Later in the evening, we had to go to the field and put them all back the way they belonged. Someone had evidently known that we were the ones who did it, told my dad, and he made us go to remedy the situation. Needless to say, we never pulled that stunt again.

We used to take chances all the time in our play and explorations, and it's amazing that one or more of us didn't get killed or maimed. I remember climbing up on the high headboard of my parents' old bed then jumping down on the bed. We did this time after time, usually with no repercussions. One time, however, I hurt my knee and couldn't walk on it for quite a long time. My sister, Irene helped me get around so that our dad wouldn't find out that I had hurt myself. Once in a while, even now, that knee will give out and I will slump down before catching myself.

We always walked on the railroad tracks, balancing flawlessly and effortlessly on the rails for long distances. We would climb onto the top of the *cupola* then slide down its slanted roof. We also climbed onto the pig shed then sat up there, chewing plug tobacco and having tobacco juice spit races to see whose stream of spittle would get to the edge of the roof first and fall off. It was up there—in addition to on top of the basement—that we sat for long stretches of time, counting and keeping track of the different cars that went by on Highway 29, just a block away from us. My sisters and I always wanted the GM cars, such as Cadillac, Chevy, Oldsmobile, or Buick, and we always tried to pawn off the Ford, Plymouth, Dodge, and Chrysler brands on Louis and our younger brothers, who didn't seem to mind. At the end of the game, we would see whose brand had the most vehicles that went by, and that person won the game. We were too naive then to know about the Saabs, Mercedes-Benz, Audi, Bentley, Jaguar, or BMW cars, and there probably weren't any of those that drove through Cadott anyway.

Sometimes, after there had been a really bad, deadly accident, which happened quite often back then, we would go down to where the crumpled vehicles were taken behind Knitter Chevrolet. We could see that area from home, on the east side of Dave Nelson's field for the cows and bulls. We walked the short distance to see the mangled cars and to absorb the seriousness and finality of driving while drunk, which was the usual cause of such tragic accidents.

We went ice fishing in the winter and into cranberry bogs to pick cranberries in the fall, both of which were fraught with dangers. We were always afraid on the bogs as sinking down with no warning can be frightening. Walking on the bogs always reminded me of being on big sponges floating on water, and I was glad when we were finished picking the berries.

One game that we played often would probably not even be allowed nowadays. We all knew how to handle and use pocketknives that we played mumblety-peg with out by the garden or wherever we could find a large flat space. We used to hold the blade of the knife and flip our wrist with a fast, strong motion to stick the blade into the ground. Whoever threw the knife the farthest and made it stick would be the winner. I think that would have been good practice for self-defense. Once in a while, we would take our mother's cooking knives, which didn't make her happy. With tools and utensils in short supply, I can see why.

Ken told me of the jokes and stunts he used to play on others. One time, he took a bicycle that belonged to one of his classmates, rode it all around, laying rubber here and there, then tied it up with a rope on the top of a flagpole. He said that people looked all over for it for a long time before finally spying it atop the pole. He would also take empty pop bottles stacked up behind one of the taverns in town, then take the bottles in to the other tavern for the few cents of deposit money. He kept going back and forth between the two taverns, gathering bottles, returning them for refund, then starting over again. Eventually, the tavern owners got wise to him, which shut down his little money-making scheme.

Ken was favored somewhat by our mother (probably because she had been so sick before his delivery), and he never wanted to be in trouble with her. He would tell our sister, "Rub, you take the blame and tell Ma that you did it," when they knew she would find out about something they did that was wrong. Then he would lay his head on Ruby's shoulder, his pleading big brown eyes begging her to get him off the hook. Ken's a charmer who, if he did not have a full beard, would look like Colin Farrell. He's the only one of us who has brown eyes instead of green or hazel.

Ken and his friend, Bobby, had a fruit jar full of cigarettes hidden under the dam. Ken rode Bobby's bike as he did not have one of his own, and Bobby used one of his brother's. Sometimes, they and other friends rode their bikes right off of the bridge and into the river, then they would retrieve them, and do it again, and none of them was ever injured during this stunt riding. They often played together in Bobby's playhouse with the fancy shutters and food.

When Ken and his friends played downtown, they often walked or ran between the buildings in the small spaces there. That would have given me claustrophobia. Some days, they would play in the stockyards that were on the north side of Hwy. 29 to the north of us. We walked past the stockyards on our way to school and town; some days, we girls played there too. We never got hurt by any of the animals, as I recall.

One time, Ken stole the lunches from some farmers and greased their old John Deere tractor. One of them told him, "Bad enough you stole our lunches, now you have grease all over!" In another tractor related incident, Ken told me about when our brother, Louis started all of the tractors at one of the dealerships in town, left them running, and ran away. When the owner found out, he removed the keys so that wouldn't happen again. Louis was always able to get things running, and as an adult could fix any old vehicle for his use.

Another incident had serious implications for a boy who was hit by a semi truck and suffered two broken legs. Ken and his friends had been throwing snowballs at each other and at the truck's windshield so the driver couldn't see. David, one of the friends, ran to get away from the snowballs and, unfortunately, into the path of the truck. The dad of Ken's friend (also named Kenny) made the two Kens go every day for a long time to do the work that their friend, David could no longer do because of his broken legs. They had to clean out the chicken coop and gather the eggs for David, as the family sold eggs as income for the family. I told Ken that because of follow-through by the other father, making them responsible and accountable for their actions, Ken grew into the fine, respectable, helpful person he is today.

Ken told me that he used to steal the tinfoil from the ragman's truck, make the foil into balls, and hide them in the crotch of the old willow tree in our front yard. He would turn these metal balls in to the ragman for a few cents. The big dog in the truck didn't stop Ken. He was fearless in his journeys through town.

Ken and his friends were mischievous rascals. One of his escapades with his friends led to eight cars of the train going off the rails. They had switched the derailers, causing the problem when the train came through later. Ken told me that a man from the Soo Line came to the house along with a policeman or FBI agent and told him that if that ever happened again he would be put away. Ken told me that he never did anything like that again.

One day my younger siblings were walking home when a truck driver stopped, opened his door, and called to them, "I'll give you each a quarter if you get in with me." Our mother had told us to ignore such an invitation, so they kept walking. We also knew to go to any door in town for help if the need ever arose, one of the advantages of living in a small town where everyone knew each other.

I wasn't directly involved in the most hair-raising, frightening event that Ruby, Marlene, and Kenny experienced. My sister Irene told me that she and I were with them also on that day, though I didn't commit that experience to memory. We lived nearly a mile from school and had to cross the train tracks four times a day, as we always went home for lunch. We were walking home from school one day and heard a train coming. Back then, the trains were pulled by those big black steam engines, a daunting specter even from a distance but more so up close. Irene told me that she and I got across the tracks but the rest weren't able to get across in time, so they thought they had to lie down between the rails. Ruby told me that Ken told her and Marlene to lie down, so they did.

Ken told me that he pushed Ruby's hand down off the rail. Why they thought that would work is desperately beyond me; however, they lived to tell about it. Ruby reported that the couplings that hung beneath the train hit their abdomens as the train passed over them. Thank God, she said, they were small enough for the train to pass over, leaving them intact. The engineer was able to stop the train and scolded them soundly. Ruby was afraid to cross the tracks after that, but had no choice.

There was a horrible and tragic train accident at the crossing on Poplar Street, just about two blocks north of where we lived, at 5:40 p.m. on May 26, 1949. A tanker truck filled with 5,400 gallons of gasoline was crossing the tracks and was hit square on by a westbound fifty-eight-car freight train and carried on the front end of the engine a long distance down the tracks. Even though I was just seven, I remember hearing the explosion that rocked the entire area and sent a big fireball into the sky that could be seen for many miles around. Several men lost their lives that day, including the driver of the truck and two railroad workers, and a fourth was critically burned. This was a devastating loss for the train line and for the people of Cadott too. Signs of the terrible accident were visible for a long time, which we saw each day we walked to and from town, reminding us of the fragility and brevity of life.

Our family was directly affected by an accident in our own home. We had come home from school for lunch one day and could see right away that something was quite wrong. When we got inside, we saw our mother holding the chipped white enamel basin that was always used for catching the blood from the pigs, but this time, she was holding it under our brother Ed's head. Somehow, he and our brother Ken, both quite small, had found the .22 rifle our dad used and that we kids learned how to shoot with also. The gun was obviously loaded still from its last use and was propped up. When it was pushed or fell over the bullet was sent in Ed's direction, grazing the lower back of his head toward the side. Luckily, it didn't penetrate very deeply. Head wounds, though, bleed profusely, so it looked really bad. Ed was not taken to the doctor, as I recall, though one of my siblings thought that he was. Ed's head healed, but I often wondered if there was some damage done because Ed has had some trouble in his lifetime from making poor choices and choosing questionable friends. A mild dysfluency has continued to be apparent in his speech, perhaps from that head trauma.

We all handled and used tools, including the cant hooks, axes, scythes and sickles and different kinds of saws, and I don't remember any of us being injured badly on any of them. We knew how to sharpen tools and knives on the grindstone and with smaller whetstones. We had to help chop the wood for both cooking and heating and became quite accomplished in that task. One time, Louis missed and chopped his foot. Luckily, it healed without stitches, which we never got when we cut ourselves. I have a scar and numbness where I cut my left index finger to the bone on a broken insulator one spring when we were damming up the creek. It took a long time for the tissue, which looked like a peeled grape, to heal.

My sister Gladie had been dancing somewhere outside the home with her other young friends and wanted to continue when she got home. She got up on top of one of our dad's old junk cars to dance some more when she fell through the back window, cutting her back, arms, and elsewhere. She told me that Louis and Irene helped to pull her out and that our dad was very angry with her. She has quite a large scar on her arm from that escapade.

One scary incident happened during the summer of 1954, after our dad had disappeared and when I was thirteen. I remember this time frame because I became aware of Benny E. who lived in the trailer court in Bateman, near Lake Wissota. I thought he was the most divine boy I had ever seen, blond, handsome, quiet, and nice, the epitome of a young girl's dream fellow. We often went swimming in Lake Wissota, entering at the far east edge of the sandy, rolling hills near the Shaffer property where it was cleared of brush, though not of the little sandburs that dug into our bare feet as we sped down to the lake. Lake Wissota would become famous decades later in the movie *Titanic*, mentioned by the character Jack Dawson, even though it had not yet been created as a source of energy by the Northern States Power Company. It has beautiful, clean, cool water perfect for swimming and cooling off on a hot, muggy day. My mother had a sister in the area and friends in Bateman, including the Shaffers who had hired Gladie to babysit and to help shovel the manure on their dairy farm, so we went there quite often to visit and to swim.

We nearly lost our mother one time on a swimming excursion. All of us kids had taken swimming lessons after our dad disappeared, and we could hold our own in the lake. Our mother, however, had never had the opportunity to learn how to swim. She must have gotten into an area where the lake dropped off, for soon we realized she was struggling. It was a frightening thing, seeing her clutching at the air and grabbing at the water to try to get her feet on the bottom once again. Louis, being a strong tall teenager, was able to rescue her by pulling her to safety using the Saint Christopher medal hanging around her neck on a secure, linked chain that she usually wore. Thank goodness she was wearing it that day, and all the links stayed connected. We usually stopped at the root beer stand on the way home for frosty, foamy mugs of root beer; on that day, the cold, sweet liquid never tasted so good.

Ruby told me of her frightening experience in our swimming area in the Yellow River. She was with her friend, Bonnie, when she had some trouble as she was learning to swim. Her friend used her new lifesaving skills and pulled her to safety onto the raft that was always out in the middle of the swimming area.

Haunted houses and old buildings are lures for children, and we were tempted by a couple of them in our area. There was an old deserted home out west of town that we explored one time, taking some items (costume rhinestone jewelry and an old mouton coat that I recall) that had evidently been left behind, thinking of them as treasures. We got in trouble later as apparently the owners had not intended to abandon the house and things inside it. We also explored another deserted house north of town. True to what one reads in novels and children's mystery books, the floors creaked, spiderwebs were everywhere, and a feeling of dread was pervasive.

West of town was where the dump was located. There was no waste management then, no organized collection of junk or garbage. There were a few local junkmen with their midsize or small trucks who went around gathering up things people no longer wanted. An older junkman, Bill Shaffer (Shakey Bill), who was a friend of my dad and a special friend of my mother too, often gave us clothes, shoes, and other things that people had thrown away. One time, he brought us a blue bike that all of us learned to ride up and down our short street. We loved playing dress up with the clothing he brought, particularly the formal gowns. We played "being really rich", especially with the nicer dresses. We stuffed old rags or stockings into bras (even though we didn't need them yet) so we would have a shape. I loved especially a light-yellow gown covered in white lace that was my favorite. Discarded, but still in good condition, high heels gave us a chance to practice getting ready to wear them for real as young ladies. It was as if we already knew Coco Chanel's philosophy about dressing: "I don't understand how a woman can leave the house without fixing herself up a little—if only out of politeness. And then, you never know, maybe that's the day she has a date with destiny. And it's best to be as pretty as possible for destiny." We were already practicing as young ladies for our dates with destiny, though not yet aware of Chanel's fashion sense.

On one occasion, we were reaching into a box, taking out things to see what, if anything, would fit each of us when we put our hands into a nest of newborn mice. They didn't even have their eyes open yet and were pink and hairless.

In addition to discarded items, Shakey Bill gave us money to go to town to get some ice cream. Generally, we got a quart, which we cut and portioned out very evenly so we all could have some. We swirled the ice cream in the small bowls, encouraging it to melt a little, and then we savored every last bit. We kids knew that Bill often gave our mother money, which she kept in a small coin purse. Without this, we may have gone hungry or without needed clothing or shoes.

The dump, with its trademark putrid smell, was above a ravine with a cave at the east end. At one time, a homeless man whose name was Wade, I think, made the cave his home. We were not afraid of him and often talked with him when we went to the dump to salvage anything that looked good that day. He cooked his food on a small stove-type contraption that consisted of a fire in a bucket with a pipe extending outside through the top of the cave for exhaust. He existed with meager material things, using candles for light, blankets and mattresses on the floor of the cave that he found at the dump, and washed his clothes in the creek. Our mother told us to "get all the useable food and good clothing you can find, and be sure to get all the shoes." Sometimes, hobos would find their way to the dump after hopping off a train. In those days, we didn't have to worry about our safety so much, though we always had others with us. There was safety in numbers then, and we were lucky to have lived in such a small village. When I told Gene about those hobos never finding their way to our house (just a short distance, two blocks from the train tracks), he said, "They probably knew that they wouldn't get anything there, anyway!"

One time, Louis, Jim, and a few others were walking back from the dump, the fruit crate filled with things that had been salvaged being slid along the rail, when Jim began to fall through the railroad ties passing over a bridge. My brother Louis grabbed the strap of his overalls and pulled him up, saving him from harm.

THE YELLOW RIVER

Just north of town is the Yellow River. We learned to swim in it, walked across its dam (a dangerous thing to do), picked ripe hops along its banks for our dad's beer, and fished many days along its edges. Fishing was one of our favorite pastimes, and it's a good thing we liked it, as often what we caught was what we ate for the next meal. Using just old bamboo poles, black line, plain hooks, and angleworms we dug out of the garden, we girls were as good at fishing as the boys. We quickly learned to tell the difference between the various kinds of fish, which ones tasted best, and where and when to catch them. We knew how to scale and clean them and often played with the air bladders that had kept the fish afloat. Taking out their entrails was not a problem for us (and we were learning biology in the process); however, we had to learn how to handle the fish to keep them from slipping out of our hands and to avoid getting pricked by their sharp fins. We also had to learn how to handle the hooks on the ends of the lines so we would not get one snagged in our flesh. We knew how to fry the fish ourselves, but occasionally, when we would catch a big redhorse (a kind of bottom-feeding sucker that is indicative of a healthy river), my mother would stuff and bake it, presenting it whole for our meal.

Irene and I were designated as the "detanglers" of the fishing lines I think because we had small, nimble fingers and the patience to do the job. It wasn't up for discussion—we were just told to straighten out the lines and we did. I remember one time that Louis got a hook stuck in his flesh somewhere, and that was a lesson for all of us as he got it out.

One time, we were walking along the bank of the river, and I lost one of my shoes to the fast-flowing water. As it was early in the summertime,

I went barefoot until the latter part of August when we all got new shoes again for school. I think that is why I have so many shoes in my closet now, because I know what it is like to be without.

We used to pick gooseberries to the west of us along the river, passing through cow pastures on the way. Sometimes, we deliberately squished cow pies between our toes, knowing that soon we could wash our feet while walking on the rocks in the shallow part of the river near the gooseberry patch. We liked to break the crust on the older cow pies and also liked to walk in the fresh ones to squeeze the manure as we walked along.

We nearly always fished in the river to the north and west of where we lived, walking through fields and brush to get there. On several occasions, we walked through nettles, which stung and burned our bare legs. One time, we had the younger kids with us. When our mother saw the younger kids jumping frenetically around, she said in an uncharacteristic choice of words, "What the hell's wrong with those kids?" I still laugh today thinking of her swearing, which she hardly ever did, and seeing kids dancing around like jumping beans was funny too, though painful. I still avoid nettles, even though naturalists recommend cooking them as tasty, early greens. I will take a pass, thank you, and keep my distance, also.

BERRY PICKING

Another favorite pastime besides fishing, which was essential for survival, was picking wild berries and other fruits. In order to find our way back out of the woods again when we were finished, my mother tied strips of rags on the bushes or trees to lead us back out, rather like Hansel and Gretel with their bread crumbs. During June, we harvested wild strawberries along the roads. July was time for luscious raspberries from patches about three miles away that my mother knew about, along with huge blueberries taken from the needle-carpeted, fragrant pine forests northwest of where we lived. August was time for blackberries (which meant lots of large, mean scratches all over our bodies in spite of the long pants and long-sleeved shirts we wore). We also picked dewberries—similar to blackberries and larger than a thumb—that grew along the train tracks. Nothing can compare to these wonderful wild fruits covered with real dairy-fresh cream after a hard day's work of walking many miles to gather them into buckets and pails and carrying them home.

One time as we were coming back with metal berry pails heavy with fruit, we climbed through a barbed wire fence as a shortcut to get home. We often did this, and we were quite skilled in navigating these shortcuts, including the ones guarded by electric fences. As I climbed through the strands of barbed wire, being careful not to catch and tear my clothing, my knee bumped the bottom of the pail I had tied around my waist. My left frontal incisor was directly in the path of the pail as it was bumped up, and the big clunk meant that that tooth would eventually die.

When I was a young mother decades later, an abscess formed above the tooth causing my face to become deformed like a monster on the left side. I didn't even look like myself, and my sons must have wondered where their mother was and who was that strange-looking creature in her place. Antibiotics brought the swelling down but the tooth could not be saved. All of my life I had liked the gap that I had between those two frontal incisors. I liked the diastema (dental term) that I had because I never got food stuck between my teeth and could win some of the contests we kids had to see whose stream of saliva could be propelled the farthest. After dental work, I missed that gap, even though my dentist (ironically, named Dr. Chulick) told me that now I had a lovely smile in place of the darkened, damaged tooth that had been there.

Decades later, my students, especially the younger ones who had changing dentition, were very interested in teeth. In addition, working as closely and as personally with students as we do in my profession, we dealt with the mouth and teeth in our work. When they would notice the silver metal behind my front teeth as I demonstrated correct placement, for example, they would always ask if they could see that bridgework, so I showed them and shared with them the cautionary lesson of always being careful with their own teeth so they wouldn't have to have metal in their mouths as I do.

Another time, in July, we came home from picking huge, juicy blueberries that we found under the pine trees on the land of my dad's friends about three miles from home. Those berries were the biggest I had ever seen, and we stuffed our mouths as we filled our pails. When we got back, our dad decided that we didn't have enough and sent us back there, even though it would soon be dark. I think that we went to the home of the friends because we certainly couldn't find berries in the dark, and in addition, it could have been dangerous out there as wild animals enjoy berries as much as we do.

One other memory about berry-picking time was shared with me by my sister Gladie. She remembered that our mother had canned berries all day and had taken the mason jars into the fruit cellar for storage. Later on that night, she was on her hands and knees, cleaning up broken jars and the fruit she had canned earlier that day. There would be that much less fruit for the wintertime.

We knew of several springs, which we drank from with a small tin cup or dipper on our way to and from the berry patches. No bottled or filtered water we use today can match the special cooling effects of such a spring, especially as most of them in the area were flowing freely all the time, and many of the wells were artesian. Crab apples, chokecherries, transparent apples, gooseberries, currants, elderberries, grapes, and hazelnuts (and even hops for my dad's homemade beer) were harvested as they were ready. My mother told me that in addition to demanding Gladie's babysitting money as soon as she got off the bus from Shaffer's, my dad often took the berries we had picked and sold them at the tavern for beer. After we had our fill of the fruits in their fresh state, my mother canned them for winter use or preserved them as jams and jellies. One year, during grape-jelly-making time, my brother Ken, as an inquisitive youngster, pulled the kettle of hot jelly down, spilling it on his chest, causing a painful burn and the scar he carries today.

We picked wild asparagus each spring and early summer and took the sprigs to Mrs. Liddell. We knew that she and her husband, Earl, liked asparagus, so we were always glad to do that for them. My mother, ironically, never cooked asparagus for us, even though there was a lot of it, free, though I wish that she would have. Evidently she didn't like it, so we never got a taste of it either. Just like lamb, we never had that either. We did have mutton, however, which was abominable. It stank as bad as wet, dirty wool.

ENTERTAINMENT

My mother took us to the free shows in Cadott each Friday night in the summertime. These shows were usually cowboy shows like *Hopalong Cassidy*, *Gene Autry*, or *Roy Rogers and Dale Evans* or shows like *Ma and Pa Kettle*. We didn't see any extravaganzas. We sat on wooden boards that were on legs, some of them rickety, and we were nearly eaten alive by mosquitoes each time we went, especially if it was humid and sweltering. We liked going anyway and looked forward to getting an ice cream cone before the show. Each scoop of ice cream cost five cents, and we knew we were living right when we got two of them for only a dime. Having to walk home afterward, especially if we had fallen asleep during the show, was difficult, but did not prevent us from looking ahead to the next week's show. We always had to get home before our dad did because he would have been angry at us for having been gone from home.

For a number of years, the Harry Brown Tent Shows came to town for several days at a time. They set up not far from where we lived, and it was a special treat to go to take in the shows. I loved the smell of the candy they sold that permeated the entire area, and for a long time I could not identify it. Finally, when I was older, I figured out that the haunting aroma of so long ago was that of rum. These boxes of candy always had some little trinket or toy inside, similar to what Cracker Jacks had in them.

We went to the Northern Wisconsin District Fair in Chippewa Falls after my dad was no longer around. We found this exciting and expanding, and we were exposed to all sorts of things that today would not be allowed. For example, I remember seeing human fetuses floating in fluid inside big jars, at all stages of development, all in sequential order. We saw all sorts of grotesquely deformed animals too, all preserved in liquid and displayed in big glass jars. There was the "bearded lady," the "wolfman," dancing women (that kids weren't allowed in to see), midgets and dwarfs, contortionists, tattooed people, sword swallowers and snake handlers, and other oddities for our curious eyes and minds. Some of those oddities back then are run-of-the-mill now, such as tattooed people and snake handlers. Carnival glass dishes, which are quite valuable and collectible now, were available in large numbers to the lucky people who could toss their coins directly onto the dishes without them sliding off. If your coin landed on or in a dish, you got to take that one home with you.

CHURCH

After my dad was gone, we were able to go to church. We attended services in various denominations before my mother settled on the Catholic church, which her family belonged to. I remember attending Easter Sunday services at the Methodist church one spring with my best friend, Jeanne. What a freeing, uplifting experience that was, with freshness and new promise all around. We also went a number of times to the small building on the west side of Main Street that housed the church of people who were commonly called the Holy Rollers, but the formal name of the church was the Gospel Tabernacle. That was eye-opening, with the exuberant enthusiasm, vigorous and vociferous singing, and some people getting carried away to the point of "witnessing" for the Lord and sharing their stories of salvation with the congregation. We also attended religious services in the homes of some people when I was just a little kid and remembered being put to sleep on a bed and then carried out after the services were finished. I just couldn't stay awake at that point in my life for endless singing and worshipping.

When my mother decided that she would indeed go back to St. Rose of Lima, we kids were excited about that. The formal beauty of the old church, the rituals, and the structure of the Mass were all interesting to us. All of us kids were baptized together, and shortly after that, Irene, Ruby, and I made our First Communion and were all confirmed together too. Our neighbor, Mrs. Lancette, who lived at the beginning of our street, was the sponsor for all of us, and we all chose confirmation names of saints we admired and intended to follow. Saint Anastasia, known as a healer, was the saint I chose to emulate.

There was a time during my high school years when I strongly considered becoming a nun, and a number of us were taken to the convent in Superior to gather more information about that type of contemplative life. I wrestled with that issue, ultimately deciding that I would live a regular life, not one of constant "poverty, chastity, and perfect obedience." I had had enough of poverty. In addition, I wanted a family of my own and I loved children, so I walked down that path at that time in my life. In my chosen profession, even though I didn't heal as St. Anastasia had, I did help and did my best to assist others with communication and hearing challenges.

MOTHER, TEACHERS, AND SCHOOL

I don't know how my mother cared for all nine of us and did her work too. Still, she made time for games and language instruction. I give thanks to my mother for instilling in me the skills needed for my professional career. Even though my mother may have been considered untalented by some, her skills as an early-language teacher were remarkable. Her excellent memory allowed her to recite at will every nursery rhyme, song, story, and game in her repertoire. She was also good at history and geography and took great pride in scoring a perfect paper on her eighth-grade examination. My mother often said that she wanted to go to high school; however, young ladies at that time were not encouraged or allowed to become educated. Usually, they married young, had their babies, worked hard, and died, leaving no legacy except their offspring. My mother often visited me while I was at the University of Wisconsin in River Falls, and a perpetual scholarship is now in her name there, so in essence, she will be in college forever. She would like knowing that.

MR. LLOYD COLLINS
Grades Seven-Eight, General
  Mathematics
Taylor County Normal
University of Wisconsin
Wisconsin State College,
  Eau Claire

MISS LILA FREESE
Grades Five-Six
Wisconsin State College,
  Eau Claire

MRS. NONA SHERMAN
Grades One-Two
Wisconsin State College,
    Eau Claire

MRS. EUNICE LIDDELL
Grades Three-Four
Wisconsin State College,
    Eau Claire

Mrs. Sherman & Mrs. Liddell on playground with students early 1950s.

Along with my mother as my first teacher and books to read that Irene brought home for me before I went to school, I always felt fortunate that we kids in Cadott had excellent teachers in school. Each teacher at the grade school level taught two grades, with a small number of students in each. For example, there were eight students in my grade, one of whom was my sister Irene who had been retained because she had trouble learning. Irene told me that her entire class was held back that year because there wouldn't have been enough students, so they were combined with my class. I don't know if that is so or not. She told me when we were grown-up that I did most of her work for her as it was quite easy for me and nearly impossible for her. I read her books and wrote the reports because she had difficulty with those skills. She also told me that I would write answers on the palm of my hand and show those to her while we were taking a test. I didn't remember that until she jogged my memory about it. Numbers were not too high because there was an elementary parochial school in town also. Mrs. Sherman, Mrs. Liddell, Miss Freese (later to become Mrs. McConville), and Mr. Collins were respected and loved by all of us. My teachers helped me to achieve and believed in me, telling my mother often that I ought to go on to college because I had the ability. Mr. Collins told my mother one time during a conference with me present, "This is one girl who ought to go on to college." Education could be my ticket out of poverty as I was blessed with a good brain. I just had to be safe until I could grow old enough to get to college.

We had to walk to school about eight-tenths of a mile from home, which was not difficult except in subzero weather. Sometimes, on those exceedingly cold days, we would try to time our departure so we could catch a ride with the music teacher who lived in our area of town. Ruby remembered our mother giving us a bed sheet to wrap around the outer perimeter of all of us walking together, with the bigger kids outside and the smaller ones inside, much as the emperor penguins do in Antarctica. We made this walk four times each school day as we went home for lunch until school lunches became available. We found this walking time to be a time of exploration and wonder, and occasionally, we got into some kind of mischief.

Gladie told me that she and some friends dug snakes out of the creek and put them in the teacher's desk, in addition to putting tacks on the seat. Kids did such things back then, but I don't remember ever playing such tricks on people I loved and admired. We would pick the early irises out of the telephone operator's yard, dam up the creek with stones, sticks, or broken insulators (that can cut a finger to the bone, I know), or hide a bottle of whiskey that we had found along the road under a small bridge. We mistakenly believed that the whiskey would keep us warm if we each took a little sip of it on the way to school. I wonder if any of our teachers ever smelled that on our breath.

Along with having the gift of being able to read, being in school was my salvation. I found it to be a place we were accepted even though we were poor and came from a family that today would probably be labeled white trash. Our teachers enabled us to be the best we were capable of being; some of us had an easier time of it than others. My mother always supported the teachers and encouraged us to do our best. Gladie's best earned her a fifty-dollar war bond when she was in high school. She had written an essay about the town of Cadott and was awarded first place and the bond. Our dad took the bond and drank it up.

Our teachers considered themselves a part of the community and were involved with us even outside of school. Mr. Collins took us quite a few times to shows in either Stanley or Augusta. We saw Mogambo and other such adult movies, as we were considered old enough to see them back then. We used to get a kick out of watching Mr. Collins eat an apple on the bus after he first showed us how to split an apple with just our thumbs pulling it apart. He ate the whole thing, stem, seeds, and even those sharp little portions that surround the seed pockets and scratch the back of your throat. We all liked Mr. Collins very much. For my siblings and me, he was a father figure in addition to being our teacher. He helped me a great deal in developing my pragmatic language skills with his weekly lessons in horse sense (identifying problems and determining solutions to them and ways to avoid such problems in the future).

SCHOOL DAYS 1954-55
CADOTT

Mrs. Liddell's 3rd & 4th grades. Irene to far right; Bev second row
from right, fifth in row. Jeanne is in front of row, arms on desk

Early 1950s; Back, L to R: Irene, Bev, Ruby, Ken;
Front, L to R, Marlene, Ed, Jim

Note what proper students we were!
Bev right up front; Irene is in row behind me, wearing glasses

Ruby, second from right, right side

Row One (l. to r.): R. Kuehni, B. Bosinske, R. Couey, R. Mattson.
Row Two: L. Brouillard, D. Western, D. Greene, T. Vlasnik, N. Boyea, G. Greene, E. Dressler.
Row Three: D. Emerson, D. Glasshoff, F. Rotermund, K. Clark, E. Peterson.
Standing: J. Loomer, I. Warner, C. Nichols, I. Bosinske, A. Christensen.

GRADES

Irene & Bev in Mrs. Liddell's room. Bev, far left row, second from front with pony tails; Irene standing, second from right

Row One (l. to r.): S. Clark, P. Peterson, N. Greene, B. Monroe.
Row Two: J. Bremness, G. Brouillard, R. Mattson, D. Thom.
Row Three: S. Falkenberg, L. Bushland, A. Klatt.
Standing: S. Dressler, J. Loomer, R. Bosinske, D. Koehler, G. Rubyor, B. Gruner, K. Hichethier, K. Jaenke, D. Kuehni, A. Bushland, N. Jahr, J. Anderson, B. Couey.

Ruby at blackboard, third from left

My mother did the best she could to make sure that we went to school clean and neat. She always combed and braided our hair, and sometimes, we curled our hair, using rag strips that we had torn off old dish towels or pillowcases. We had limited clothing, which we had to take off as soon as we got home in the afternoon so they would stay clean and nice. We had to wear those plain long tan stockings instead of the nice white ones that other girls wore because they were less expensive. These stockings were held up with strong, thick bands of elastic above our knees, which often were too tight and left long-lasting, itchy indentations in our thighs.

We had just one pair of shoes, bought in August at Dupey's, the local shoe store, or at Dietrich's, the local general store. One year, Irene told me, she had to wear Louis's old shoes or his old black rubber boots with the buckles up the front because she didn't have any of her own. Our mother scolded us sometimes when we walked down the counters in the backs of the shoes and always tried to get us to be very careful with the shoes so they would last all school year. We had those old-fashioned high-topped shoes some years, which were harder to damage and would therefore last longer. When the soles were worn through, we put cardboard in the bottoms to keep our feet off the ground. Boots that got rips or cuts in them were repaired with rubber cement and patches and continued to be used.

We always walked to school, generally going the back way as our dad told us not to go down Main Street. Sometimes we did, though, and we always checked things out on our walk. There was a cheese factory owned by the Hamms right across the street to the west of the school. I remembered many times watching the whey flow down the side of the tank or vat which was about as tall as a barn silo. The smell from the factory did not seem to interfere with our learning, and we found it interesting to observe a part of the cheese-making process. We never went there to take a closer look, however.

We liked being in school where we were safe and among friends and caring teachers. We had a rigorous school day, going from eight until four, broken up by a lunch period that was about a full hour long, with enough time for recesses in the morning, noon hour, and afternoon. We played outside in all kinds of weather, even the severe below-zero days, and our teachers were right out there with us. Our wet mittens were placed on top of the old radiators to dry before we needed them again, and our coats, boots, and other gear were kept in the cloakroom at the back of each classroom. One time, when I came back from lunch at home and was removing my things, Mrs. Sherman saw all the other items strewn around on the floor, assumed that I had done that, and grabbed me by the hair, pulled me up, and shook me, scolding me because she thought that I was the culprit when I wasn't.

We learned all the basics, including phonics and spelling, reading with Dick and Jane, proper grammar and pronunciation, basic arithmetic, and the Palmer Method of cursive writing. We also had time for the creative activities such as screen painting, using a loom, weaving, and other arts and crafts. We had regularly scheduled time slots throughout the year when we were all expected to perform for our class at the front of the room, such as singing a song, reciting a poem, or something similar. I was very excited when I learned "Mockingbird Hill" to sing when it was my turn. My mother helped me to learn all the verses and the melody. I was nervous, but I did remember all the words.

When school was over, some of us, especially my sisters and I, almost always stayed and helped our teachers clean and wash the blackboards and clap the erasers outside, sometimes banging them against the brick building or sidewalks. We also helped with other jobs to get ready for the next day of school before heading home. School was a welcome respite and a haven compared to the chaos and anger of our dad that we often went home to.

In addition to the academics, we also liked being at school because that was where there were many pieces of playground equipment to play on. We all liked the big metal slide, of course, and the teeter-totters and were skilled in figuring out how to balance so that we could stay perfectly still at times. We would pull and jerk the heavy planks of wood into one of the three curved sections where the heavy metal attached to the planks fitted onto the support portion of the teeter-totters, figuring out how to equalize partners who weighed different amounts. We were always careful to warn the other person that we intended to get off so he or she could be ready for stopping too.

One of our pieces of equipment was a merry-go-round that spun very fast, and we were careful to help others on and off. I don't remember any accidents; however, nowadays, such equipment is considered dangerous for kids and hardly ever found on a playground. Our favorite area to play in was over by the chains. This contraption was a tall metal pole in the middle with about six chains hanging from the top. These each had three grips spaced out that we hung on to as we ran around then swung free for as long as possible, enjoying the ride. We always called out to the others who were also swinging that we wanted to get off so they could all be prepared for a change or if other kids wanted to get on. Getting hit with one of the heavy chains could have caused a serious injury; however, I don't remember any of us getting hurt on them.

At the end of each school year, there was always a picnic at Irvine Park in Chippewa Falls. We all went there by bus, spending all day there. We walked around, tried to see the bears that lived there in the cave, and especially liked swinging on the tall swings. We thought that we pumped them so hard that they actually went over the top of the bar. Now, as an adult, I don't know if that is possible or not, but we thought that we did it back then. Maybe it was our spirits that went over the top, not us; however, regardless of what it was, we soared the entire day. Lunch was always delicious, provided by everyone bringing something. Our mother was always assigned the task of providing the paper plates. I suppose that was because our food resources would have been sparse and the teachers knew that, and maybe they wouldn't have trusted food that came out of my mother's kitchen because we had no running water, and they may have been suspicious of sanitation.

At the end of the school year, we spent the better part of one day cleaning up all the trash on the large school grounds and along the streets by the school. We worked in teams, collecting the junk in bags. We learned early to respect Mother Nature and to keep things neat and clean, not like today when litter is strewn everywhere by people who have no concept of honoring the great gifts we have been blessed with. Afterward, we enjoyed a picnic and games to celebrate another good year and the beginning of the summer.

WRONG BEHAVIOR

It must have been because we felt deprived or hungry that we often stole items from the local grocery store. Mr. Ruff and his employees must have known that it was we who took the bananas and the chocolate baking bars (ironically named Baker), and Mr. Miller must have known that we were the ones who took small pieces of penny candy from his drugstore on the days we didn't have any change. Sometimes, I remember looking at all the different kinds of candy before choosing then paying for my choice when I had coins. It was a good feeling to pay for something instead of stealing it.

Some of the wrong behavior was encouraged, in fact ordered, by our dad. He would make Louis go to other people's clotheslines and take items off to bring home. Not a very good example or role model for young kids. It seemed to me that Louis was always getting in trouble from an early age. Ken was lucky that he had been channelled into proper behavior by his friend, Kenny's dad and the railroad official and man of the law.

The Marcotts, who ran the local bakery, were very good to us. They always gave us the leftover rolls and bread and other baked goods rather than throw them away. Those were wonderful, and we appreciated the thoughtfulness of the Marcotts. We never stole anything from their business.

CUSTODIAN

There's only one "Red"
Bates! His furnace keeps
our bodies comfortable;
his smile warms our hearts.

The most brazen thing we did as kids that was definitely wrong was to get into the school and steal cases of Coke from the basement near Mr. Bates's office. Mr. Bates, the janitor of the school, was called Red probably because of the color of his hair when he was young. He must have known it was "the Bosinske tribe" that had sneaked in and taken the Coke. We got in through the coal bin more than once, if I remember correctly, and took the Coke up under the train viaduct southeast of the school to savor the cool, refreshing wonder in the shapely green bottles with the slim neck. No soda today tastes as good as the pop back then. One of my sisters told me that school officials had seen us, came to the viaduct where we were, told us that what we did was wrong, and told us that if we wanted pop, we could have just asked for it. I don't know if any of our thefts were reported to our mother or not. People probably knew that she couldn't watch us every minute of the day. In addition, she was known as a good person who did her best with many kids and a mean, drunken husband.

This is how we lived until October of 1957, when our social worker determined that it would be better for us kids to be placed in homes that were different from our own. My friend Big Bev once described our living situation as "*Peyton Place* run amok." Obviously, the social worker must have thought that our mother had been unable to protect either Gladie or Irene and that I or my younger sisters could be next. With our family trait of submissiveness, we were targets for subjugation. The attack on our sister Irene and the constant threat from Crazy George led to this life-changing decision and took me to Glenwood City and the Rivards and on my path of my lifelong dream of getting out of poverty, becoming a respected person, and doing good things to help others.

Part II:
Glenwood City
and River Falls

LIVING IN HEAVEN

Living with the Rivards was like moving on to heaven compared to the poverty and hardship I had grown up in and known all my life. There was work, to be sure, but having walls of books, fine art, and music to appreciate was more than an even trade-off. Best of all, no Crazy George to worry about. Here, I was safe.

My new family (a few years after I went to live with them).
Back, L to R: Louis, Andre`, Rollie, Franny;
Front: L to R: Richard, Ray, Michelle, Georgie, Mary

The striking red house, traditional inside and out, and set on several acres, surrounded by many more at the northwest edge of town, was large and welcoming. Inside, everything was in order as Mary was very organized. There were large rooms downstairs, living, dining, den/library, bedroom, kitchen, one bathroom that was the only one in the house at that time, and another bedroom that was used as the work room for ironing, washing, drying, and folding mountains of laundry and polishing all those shoes. This room would eventually be made into a new kitchen, while keeping the old and adding a wood-burning stove to that first kitchen, which became the area for warming up after a day of cross-country skiing or other outside activity. The initial bathroom would become part of the new kitchen, and another bathroom would be incorporated into the master bedroom.

The upstairs had three bedrooms, one of them very large, and multiple large attic spaces, all neatly organized. Some of those attic spaces eventually were made into another bathroom and one more bedroom with stained glass, salvaged from a church, to catch the rays of the setting sun.

The main, formal entrance to the house was at the large front door where I first saw Franny with his dimpled face and met Mary. A full-length porch ran the entire length of this side of the house which faced County Highway G. Another entrance was the back door near the kitchen, and the third, through the "garage," a portion of the basement that had a very steep slope. Richard would drive up to the double doors, pull on a heavy weight tied to a rope at his left side through the open car window, then grin at his genius in this design while waiting for the doors to open like the gates of heaven. Going down this incline was like a carnival ride, then the quick stop to prevent crashing into the wall at the other end. I always worried that one time the brakes would fail, but they never did. I drove down this slope just a few times and never enjoyed the thrill of the risk as Richard obviously did. And yes, there was always the ever-present, hearty laugh Richard was known for. If I had to synthesize Richard into one characteristic, it would have to be his all-out laugh as that was his very essence. Such joie de vivre!

Eventually, there would be a new addition at the edge of the old kitchen that served as a new garage, and the old garage would become the area for the hot tub used in the winter.

The basement, outside of the garage area, was used as a playroom, workbench area, canned-food storage area, and eventually Mary's office, and a replaced laundry center. In addition to his "Rube Goldberg" heating system, at one time Richard had his hi-fi or stereo area down there so that he could fully enjoy, sometimes at full blast, listening to his classical music. He especially liked to listen to Ravel's *Bolero* or Tchaikovsky's *1812 Overture*, which he marched around to while pumping his arms, emphasizing the strong beats of the music. Occasionally, we joined him in his march of total enjoyment, even as adults, and my sons joined right in with the merriment, especially when the cannon blasts appeared in the music. In the warm-weather season, two huge speakers were placed outside so that the music could be enjoyed no matter where one was. The people downtown, about a mile or so away, could probably enjoy it too. No one ever complained, though, at least to my knowledge.

Andre` & Brian, early 70s, by repurposed chicken coop, now the beer house

My family, 8-11-96 by beer house,
L to R: Darren, Gene, my mother, Brian, Bev, Sean, Brendan

A chicken coop that had been repurposed as a beer house was at the right side of the first entrance of the driveway. While I was with the Rivards, Mary painted the outside with swedish rosemaling, a beautiful, swirly, floral pattern that she excelled at. She transformed the old chicken coop into a cozy, inviting beer house that was frequented many times through the years by family, friends, hangers-on, and young tasters, surreptitiously sampling their first taste of the brew. The same rosemaling on the beer house decorated the doors of the kitchen cabinets, which I believe are still there in the house that is now a bed-and-breakfast.

There would be a swimming pool and sauna to look ahead to also the next summer. Richard had a large, self-designed pool made of asphalt that was painted every few years. My friend and college roommate, Erma, and I had this job one summer. Needless to say, we were glad when we were finished as that was a tricky job. With the sloping sides, significant depth at the diving end, and tar between our toes to contend with, it was a good job done. With a sloping angle at one end and deep enough at the other to accommodate diving off a wooden diving board, the pool provided many days of summer fun for the entire community, especially the kids.

It was where I spent many of my days watching over them. Glenwood's own pool was rather like a sandpit, but it was also used by the kids from town. My own sons looked forward each summer to going up to Glenwood for the resortlike atmosphere and welcoming family time. They rode in the back of the Volvo station wagon with no restraints at all, as that was before seat belts became mandatory, often sleeping on the way.

Along with the pool at this end of the property, Richard and his helpers had also built a bathhouse (properly divided into Boys and Girls), a sauna, a shower area, and the area he proudly wrote over the doorway, *La toilette*—a nod to his French Canadian heritage.

Richard made all the improvements to his property by himself and the young men he could convince to help him. They were always glad to help as that meant that they could then swim, have a beer if old enough, and use the sauna later. The sauna was lined with cedar and had an upper and a lower bench. A firebox fired up with wood at the outside heated up the rocks upon which someone would pour a small amount of water to provide steam. When that happened, Richard always let go a peal of laughter, relishing his clever ingenuity. After such a steamy session, it was time to run and dive off the diving board to cool the body and replay this entire scenario. If it was wintertime, there would be a roll or a run in the snow to cool off. Always, Richard's, the guests', and the kids' laughter filled the air.

There were a number of jobs that were my responsibilities with my new family. I did most of the cooking, which I enjoyed and was already quite proficient at, thanks to my home ec classes each year. Mary always planned the menus and saw to it that the shelves in the basement, the refrigerator, and the storage shelves in the kitchen were well stocked. Mary is an excellent cook herself, just as her mother, Grandma Jensen, was. To this day, I use many of their recipes and techniques, along with some of my mother's and sisters'. Dishes had to be washed, dried, and put away after each meal in order to keep up with all of them. With ten people around the table, there were many dishes all the time, not counting all the drop-in guests who were frequent. And of course, at that time, dishwashers were not in most home kitchens.

Richard and Mary entertained quite often as they were leaders in the community and had many obligations to fulfill in their church and political party. Entertaining on a large scale was often handled outside in the nice weather. A large stone barbecue pit, constructed by Richard and his helpers, was covered by a couple of recycled grills off one thing or another. Cooking massive amounts of food, especially chicken or pork chops for all the guests, could easily be done on this barbecue. Big pancake breakfasts, including bacon and sausage on a large griddle, were often the highlight of a summer Sunday morning. Richard's door was always open to nearly everyone, and many meals and kegs of beer were shared in storytelling and laughter, sitting around on the lawn or in the beer house.

I cleaned the house every Saturday, the entire upstairs, and helped with the downstairs. All the leather shoes were polished at least every week as tennis shoes were only worn on the gymnasium floors at school. The shoes were lined up in pairs on newspaper, polish applied, buffed with an old diaper or other soft cloth, then shined even more with a brush. I was glad when liquid shoe polish was invented, thus saving a lot of time. I helped with the laundry also and the ironing, which in those days was of some consequence, as most items were ironed to look their best. It was very different from today when items are rarely, if ever, ironed and kids' socks are not even matched anymore. No one home to do those tasks, I presume.

Curtains throughout the house were washed at least twice a year or more often if needed. The lace panels that covered the lower portions of the windows were stretched on special devices with sharp little metal pegs, like nails that had their heads cut or filed off, all along the edges before being placed in the sunshine to dry. All curtains needed ironing, except for the lace curtains which had been totally straightened out by the aggressive stretching.

Mary did the worst job in the house entirely by herself. Every spring, she removed the furniture from each room with hardwood floors. Using turpentine solvent, she scraped every smidgen of old wax and varnish off the wood, then thoroughly washed by hand, on hands and knees, every inch of the floors. After drying, a fresh coat of varnish was applied. It was allowed to dry completely, and then a second coat was applied. The person or pet who made tracks on a partially dried section of varnish would see a force to be reckoned with. This entire procedure took a number of days, and we were all glad when it was over so that we could resume normal patterns of traffic, and the strong petroleum vapors and odor would have dissipated.

In 1958 or '59, Richard purchased The Glen, the theater on the main drag of town. On the outside of the front, there were large glass doors that opened to allow changing of the movie posters (now quite valuable, I understand). Andre` and Rollie learned to operate the big old reel-to-reel projector up in the projection booth, and I helped sell tickets, popcorn, and other goodies for the patrons. We saw nearly every movie on the large, wide screen, but long after they were in larger cities and no longer new. Working at the theater was handy for us as we got to see many of our friends, some of whom were allowed to sneak in. We had to help with the cleaning also. It was a tricky job to get the debris from under all those seats while sweeping the floors, including the floor in the balcony.

Large five-gallon buckets, stored in a little section at the side of the screen, contained the palm oil used in popping the corn that was buttered lavishly with real butter. The oil used back then was natural, delicious, and much better than most oils used today. I had a problem with this oil one night in the summer of 1960, which was entirely my own fault. After all the crowd had begun to watch the movie, I put some of the solid white oil into the corn popper to melt to pop another batch, then left to pick up items that had been dropped in the doorways and elsewhere in the lobby. Time went by faster than I realized, for soon I smelled hot, burning oil in the lobby. Not thinking and not using the scientific principles I had learned in my science classes, I foolishly lifted the Pyrex measuring cup up to the kettle, tipping the kettle until the hinged lid fell away. I thought that the melted oil would pour into the cup where it could cool. Wrong! You know what happened. That's right, immediate combustion from the air that entered the kettle and hot oil and fire all over my dominant hand holding the cup.

Grabbing the full skirt of my aqua-and-white toile scooped-neck dress that I always loved to dance in, I quickly wrapped my hand in the fabric to put out the flames after pulling off my class ring (which I never found). One of the patrons took me to the clinic just a block or so away where Dr. Limberg treated me and wrapped my hand in gauze like a big boxing glove. When I got home, I asked Mary for a cigarette—my coping mechanism at that time for the traumatic injury I had brought upon myself. I had to go periodically to have the hand debrided of all the dead, sloughing tissue and a new bandage applied. This club of a hand now necessitated that I learn how to do everything with my left hand. In eight weeks, the length of time it took for my hand to heal, I got quite skilled in writing, doing my hair, grooming, applying makeup, cooking, and performing all other life skills with my left hand. I am lucky that there are no residual problems from my carelessness.

Summer trip out west, 1960,
Front: L to R: Richard, Franny, Louis, Rollie, Bev, Andre`;
Back: Michelle (behind her, Georgie and/or Ray, I think)

There was one major trip that I was on with all the Rivards, a camping trip to Rapid City, South Dakota, into Cheyenne, Wyoming, then on to Denver and Colorado Springs in the summer of 1960. All ten of us traveled in Richard's big old Pontiac station wagon, the one that looked like a land yacht with wooden panels on the sides. Richard, of course, was in the driver's seat, Mary sat beside him in the passenger's side in front, and the rest of us in the back however we could fit in, as I recall, as there were no seat belts or laws then to restrain (or protect) us. This worked out quite well, and most of the time, we got along well and had no problems. The worst that happened was when Michelle, Franny, or I got motion sickness, and of course, all at different times. Those mountain roads were the worst. But there were so many new things to see. So we all made the best of it and adapted. I don't remember anyone ever complaining about us being sick and hindering them (bless them).

Richard had diligently and carefully planned the entire trip months ahead of time, which he did for all the trips that his family took. Mary, organized as she was, had planned outfits for all of us, packed up in sets, which we changed every two days. She also planned all the food and menus along the way. She cooked with a Coleman stove, often by hanging-lantern light. Showers were at the campsites, taken quickly, especially if there wasn't much warm water. With such a large family, camping was the way to go that was affordable and popular at the time. Later, Richard had a couple of different RVs (recreational vehicles) such as Arrow or Winnebago that he drove all over the country, including up into Alaska. Richard loved to travel and loved talking other people into going along with him on his adventures.

There was just one big argument on that trip. Andre` and I, who usually got along very well, (and still do) were helping to set up the tent. I don't know what started it, probably frustration with those gosh darned tent stakes, or maybe where the tent would be located, but we got into a heck of a row. That blew over, though, and during that trip along one of those beautiful mountain rivers or streams, in nature's majestic arms, we celebrated Andre` becoming a teenager.

We nearly lost Georgie on this trip, and I can see her in my mind as clearly as if it were today. There she was right up on the ledge, fearless, high above the Royal Gorge, looking and stretching down. It could have been heart-attack time. Mary calmly and quietly went up to her, took hold of her, and helped her down. It took a long time for the scared feelings to leave us; however, Georgie, always laughing like her dad, did not realize the gravity of her situation.

Being in the Rivard household was never dull as there was always some kind of activity or another. I liked all the kids very much (in fact, I loved them, still do), and we got along very well. Only occasionally would I have to chase after them with the wooden spoon, maybe for such an infraction as getting into some of the cookies or food that we had already prepared for company or one of Mary's women's club meetings. During those times when I would play with them and kid around, I would tell them that I knew jiu jitsu so they had better behave and I think that they believed me. I really didn't know any of the martial arts, I just told them that to have a little leverage over them. Sometimes I would play that I was Frankenstein's Monster, walking toward them stiff legged and with arms outstretched. I think that Georgie actually was afraid of "Frankie" but not the other kids. The kids all thought of me as one of the family and always introduced me to their friends as "my big sister, Bev." When I told my students many years later about how many siblings I had, their eyes would get big when I told them that I had fifteen altogether. If my students happened to have been adopted, my having lived in a foster home was reassuring to them that their life could turn out OK too.

Holidays with the Rivards were always celebrated lavishly and in warm fellowship. We either entertained at home or spent the special days with Richard's brother, Ray, and his wife, Annabelle, who lived on a farm near Turtle Lake or with the Jensens, Mary's mother and her husband, Cliff. I liked going to Grandma Jensen's, but always had some difficulty tolerating the strong cigar odor that permeated the entire house. Grandma Jensen was a very good cook, and she did everything in style, with elegant dishes, linens, and presentations. She smoked too but cigarettes instead of cigars. She did have a very unique skill that I liked to see her perform, which was blowing large, full streams of smoke through both flared nostrils at the same time, rather like an angry dragon, except that I never saw her angry. Everyone smoked back then it seemed, except Richard. I never saw him use any tobacco products. He scolded me one time when I was in college and brought a small sample package of cigarettes and gave them to Andre`. I never did anything like that again.

Christmastime was extremely special in the Rivard home. Mary spent several weeks decorating the entire house, often with artwork she had made. Candy wreaths hung on the doors, hand-made felt or satin stockings for all the kids hung on the fireplace, and every single wall and corner of the house was decorated. It was like entering into a magical Christmas house, with baking aromas adding to the magic. We baked many different cookies and made candies for days at a time. I would come home from school, prepare supper, clean up the dishes, get the kids to bed, and then make a large batch of one of Mary's special recipes. One night, it would be swedish spritz; the next, divinity or fudge; another, toffee; another, pecan rolls; another, russian tea cakes (my personal favorite).

Brian & Bev making Russian Tea Cakes, early 2000s.

These tea cakes have been included in my own holiday baking every year since 1957 and are a favorite of all my own family and extended family as well. In fact, they are so highly prized that people have been seen sneaking and hiding them from others to keep and savor themselves. My sons always looked forward to sitting around the kitchen table, spread first with newspapers then waxed paper, upon which we placed dozens of these delectable balls of goodness, made only of a few ingredients and rolled in powdered sugar. They melt in your mouth and are best popped in all at once. I always try to make them as small as possible to stimulate this savory, nearly sinful pleasure.

Making the peanut cakes was delayed until all the kids could be assembled around the kitchen table to shuck peanuts. A lot of them. After shucking, they would be ground into small pieces by peanut grinders that were turned with little handles, rather like those found on a jack-in-the-box or an old organ grinder. Either Mary or I would have baked a yellow rectangular cake that was cut into small pieces. These small pieces were frosted with plain white frosting then rolled into the ground peanuts, covering all sides. Now, of course, you ended up with a fat, globby chunk that had to be cut down again and again, refrosted and rerolled as many times as needed until you ended up with a small,

manageable delicious bite to place into the mouth in one piece. Rollie
has kept this cooperative tradition alive. I think he's the only one with
the patience to do it.

All of these baked goods or candies were packed in small decorative
tins and then hidden in one of the cool attic spaces upstairs. Occasionally,
somebody in the house got into the goodies and sampled them ahead of
time. We usually knew who the guilty one was by what was taken as we
knew which treats were the favorites of all the kids.

Christmas of 1957 was the first "real" Christmas I ever had. It was
wonderful in every way. We sat around listening to Christmas music,
enjoyed oyster stew and a tuna casserole, then rested or napped until it
was time for all of us to attend midnight Mass. This was an elaborate,
uplifting, long service made special by the lateness of the hour, the
beautiful hymns, and the magic of the season.

Under the big tree that went nearly to the ceiling were piles of gifts
that Mary had been getting or making and wrapping for weeks ahead
of time. The kids would sit nearby, trying to guess what was in each
package, especially if it had their name on it. My gifts were all very nice,
things that I needed, such as my first bathrobe, a pretty pink one, a few
items of clothing, small costume jewelry, a tube of lipstick, a hairbrush, a
diary, gold-and-white hand-knit mittens, and a red cable-knit head cover
all made with love by Mary (that I still have), a box of stationery. After
an early Christmas morning breakfast, including hot chocolate enjoyed
out of Santa mugs, we all sat around while Andre`(usually) acted as
Santa to deliver the gifts one at a time so that we all knew who got what
from whom. This entire gifting session went on for quite a long time.

For my graduation, Mary planned two parties for me: one, a "hi-fi"
party for my classmates and the other for family. Grandma Jensen
bought me a lovely full-skirted pastel-pink dress, and Mary made me
a classic sheath of white cotton piqué. I found new heels that were cut
low on the outside of the foot with a low throat and were quite elegant.
Miss Hartfiel gave me a light-blue sweater clip designed like flowers that
I wore for many years. Wonderful memories of that time.

During the time that I stayed with Richard and Mary, not all times
were easy. I often would break down into crying jags that lasted a long
time, leaving me with red, swollen eyelids and a thoroughly dragged-out
feeling. Mary, mainly, had the painstaking job of helping me work
through my problems. She was patient with me, though I'm sure it
wasn't easy.

I rarely had to be disciplined by Richard or Mary; however, one time Richard and I got into a strong disagreement about the quality of music popular at the time. Richard disliked rock and roll immensely, and I supported it, danced to it, and listened to it every chance I could. In exasperation one time, he said to me, "I can't understand how someone who likes Shakespeare can like that Elvis!"

The only other time he was exasperated with me was when I was in college. My friend Erma and I had gone to a double-feature movie in Menomonie with Mike and Tom, friends in college with us in River Falls who had driven over eighty miles to Glenwood to get us. By the time both movies were finished, it was very late as outside movies at the drive-in did not begin until after dark in the summertime. We tried to sneak into the house quietly; however, Richard heard us through the open bedroom window, came storming out in his boxers and T-shirt, and read us the riot act. He was not happy that his sleep had been disturbed and that we were extremely late, with boys no less. Our friends were going to sleep in the car for a while before going on the long drive home to Lake City, Minnesota, but after observing Richard in his extremely angry and agitated state, they went on their way. Ahh, the perils of going to drive-in movies in the summertime.

FROM A HORNET TO A HILLTOPPER

On my first day in my new school, the principal, Mr. Berg, easily six-and-a-half-feet tall at least and as commanding as he was tall, introduced himself then escorted me with the fluid movements of one who had been an athlete all his life on a tour of the building. He introduced me to Sally, who would become one of my friends. She was a good student too and the same religion I was, so I suppose he thought we'd get along well, which we did.

I was placed in the same classes I had been in while living in Cadott, except there had to be a little change for Latin. Cadott was in first year Latin while Glenwood was in second year. Luckily for me, Miss Mattie Reece was the Latin teacher there. She graciously and willingly taught a class just for me all year long. She gave up an hour of her time each school day to tutor me and did it with no complaints. What an angel. The following year was the same as I was out of synch with the Glenwood schedule. Miss Reece was also the geometry teacher so I had her for that class too. Thankfully, I liked geometry best of all my math classes because it made sense to me. All my other teachers were nice too and were excellent teachers. I lucked out once again, having teachers who were doing their job because they loved it and were good at it.

Miss Reece often wedged little snippets of wisdom in among her lessons, and I have kept and memorized the one she shared with me by John Oxenham, called "The Way":

JENNINGS B. PAGE

Bachelor of Science in Education
U. of Minnesota - Duluth Branch

Graduate Work - U. of Minn.

English 11 and 12
Junior Class Advisor
Dramatics Club
Junior and Senior Class Plays

MATTIE RUTH REECE

Bachelor of Arts
Carleton College, Northfield, Minn.

Graduate Work - U. of Iowa,
U. of Washington, Drake University

English 9, Latin II, Geometry
Freshman Class Advisor

Mr. Page & Miss Reece

The Way

To every man there openeth
A Way, and Ways, and a Way,
And the High Soul climbs the High Way,
And the Low Soul gropes the Low,
And in between, on the misty flats,
The rest drift to and fro.
But to every man there openeth A High Way, and a Low.
And every man decideth
The way his soul shall go.

I was interested in continuing to be a majorette, so I went to see Mr. Clair and requested a tryout for one of the positions. I was chosen to be one of the twirlers and strutters, which is how majorettes did things back then. I was so glad to be included in the marching band, now as a Hilltopper instead of a Hornet. I had diligently, even compulsively, taught myself to twirl as a small girl, spending hours at a time, day after day, using a cut-down broom handle or a stick as I had no baton.

Majorettes

SUSAN LUECK

BEVERLY BOSINSKE

SANDRA KRIZAN

JUDY VANRANST

GLORIA HOFF

Marching Band

Bev, second from left in row of twirlers

How exciting it was to purchase my very own real baton with my babysitting money. I remember taking the Greyhound bus and going into Woolworth's five-and-dime store in Chippewa Falls, admiring all the different lengths lined up, feeling the weights at the ends, checking out the different patterns of spiraling around the length of the metal. I chose the one that was the right size for me, measuring it underneath my arm to a little beyond my fingertips to be sure it wasn't too long to twirl correctly. I was driven by something inside to learn and to master that skill, watching Marianne Stanek every chance I could as a girl in Cadott. My classmate Sandy was the head drum major in Glenwood, which was perfect as she was tall, pretty, and had good leadership ability. I was happy to be included as one of the four twirlers.

In addition to performing as a majorette, I also participated in Future Homemakers of America (FHA)—comparable to Future Farmers of America (FFA), the glee club and chorus, and speech/drama, and forensics activities. Even though I was a member of the library club and the yearbook staff in Cadott, I did not participate in those activities in Glenwood.

I learned to drive during high school, taking both the classroom session and behind the wheel. I drove during the wintertime, mainly between Glenwood and Boyceville, which was a big asset to me in later years, but Richard would not allow me to take the driving test. I think that he didn't want me out on the roads with his car. Eventually, when

I was nineteen and in college, I did take the test, having to take it twice because the first time I did not do well in parallel parking. It's hard to learn a skill well when there is no practice time and no vehicle to use.

One time I drove Richard's cream-and-coral Ford, which was a good-looking car, to River Falls for a dental appointment. On the way back, I was trying to light a cigarette and ran into a mailbox along the highway south of Glenwood. I didn't tell Richard about the small dent in the front of the car, but someone told him about the incident. They probably knew the car as it was quite distinctive and attractive. That was the only time I ever damaged any of Richard's property.

Every Monday night, those of us who attended St. John the Baptist Church had to go to catechism, called CCD classes. We had to learn the Confraternity of Christian Doctrine, and every week, we left the church with a "plan of action" intended to help us to make good choices and to live an exemplary life. Without fail, at least half of the weeks, my friends Tom and Peter, my handsome, heartthrob, athletic classmates, and I would whisper to each other across the aisle. Sure enough, portly old Father Niggemann, rigid and not straying one iota from the rules, would catch us and punish us the rest of the class time of about an hour on our knees on the hard tile floor. That didn't stop us, though. Just too much to talk and whisper about, I guess, though I couldn't tell you one thing we just *had* to whisper about if my life depended on it.

The social life I led during this time was very limited due to my delay in that area, and I did not date at all. I went to some of the dances, mainly the sock hops popular at that time, but I did not go to the prom either of my last two years of high school. I stayed home those nights, feeling a little sad and left out, but more than made up for these missed dances when I was in college and danced in very fine dance halls with amazing and exciting dance partners.

Being involved in plays was interesting to me. Mr. Page cast me in the lead role of our senior-class play; however, I don't remember the name of the play. I do remember that there were classmates backstage, making the sights and sounds of rain, lightning, and thunder at one point, so there must have been something ominous about the setting or plot. I do remember that my role was that of a young girl, so it wasn't much of a stretch, if any at all.

Those of us in home ec, nearly all of us girls even though we were on a college prep track, were involved in a style show put on each spring. There was a script, a narrator, props, and flowers. We modeled the garments we made, including the accessories we chose to accent our ensembles. I modeled my blue classic suit with white blouse and white pillbox hat popular at that time, white gloves, and matching shoes and clutch purse. Back then, hats and gloves matched, and shoes and purses were always the same color. We learned how to look our best and to be appropriate in presenting ourselves in public, and without fail, people checked out the backs of our calves to see if those seams of our nylons were absolutely straight; hair and makeup neat; gloves, especially white ones, without stain; shoes polished and clean, without run-down heels. What a difference today, when anything goes.

During the summer of 1958, our high school burned, and the following year, classes met in different locations throughout town. The elementary students met in churches while most of our high school classes were held in the elementary section of the building. This was a devastating loss to the entire town, and eventually, a new school was built midway between Glenwood and Downing, a smaller town to the southeast on the way to Boyceville.

On February 3, 1959, several of us seniors walked down town during our lunch break. It was during this time that we learned the devastating news about Buddy Holly, the Big Bopper, and Ritchie Valens. During the early morning hours of the night before, their plane had crashed in Iowa, and that was when the "music died." I learned sometime later that Waylon Jennings, not yet famous in 1959, gave up his seat to the Big Bopper. All of us teenagers were heartbroken about this loss, especially of Buddy Holly, though all three musicians would be mourned for decades. I became a big fan of Waylon, and to this day, I am glad that he was not on that plane too.

BADGER GIRLS STATE

During the summer of 1958, between my junior and senior years of high school, I was privileged to have been selected by the faculty of my high school to attend the yearly event of Badger Girls State, a week-long session of learning about our political system. This week-long event has been sponsored for over seventy years by the American Legion Auxiliary in each small town across Wisconsin. My friend Julie was selected as the alternate delegate, and I felt sad for her that I was selected instead. If I hadn't been sent to Glenwood City, she would have been chosen. I think that Mr. Flottum, one of our teachers and a friend of Richard and Mary, wanted me to have this rare chance for personal development, and maybe, I thought, he admired me for what I had already had to deal with. He did write in one of my yearbooks, "I admire your courage."

We lived right on campus, in Barnard Hall, at the University of Wisconsin in Madison. Those of us from the area of River Falls, Glenwood City, and other small towns in northwestern Wisconsin took the bus for the four-or-five-hour drive to Madison. One of my bus mates was JoAnne (Jo to us), who represented River Falls. Her father was a faculty member, and her mother was an elegant, refined librarian whom I worked with at the university when I was a student librarian as one of my part-time jobs.

When we got to Madison, we were assigned rooms, roommates, and a political party—either the Nationalists or Federalists, if I recall correctly. The party I was assigned to was different from the one Jo was assigned to, but I remember supporting her because I could tell that she was going places. She did, in fact, end up as Badger Girls State governor that year and ultimately ended up teaching literature to medical students.

Each day, we had classes to attend, caucuses to participate in, posters and campaign ads to prepare, campaigning to do, and new friends to make. We spent time in Bascom Hall and the magnificent capitol of the state of Wisconsin on the square, in addition to time in Barnard Hall. The program is considered a practical application of Americanism and good citizenship. Each night, we had vespers, a quiet, prayerful, contemplative time before retiring. These services followed a specific order and included hymns, singing, chanting, verses read aloud, prayers, and reflecting in silence.

When I returned to Glenwood, one of my obligations to the Auxiliary was to give a speech about my experiences to the entire group. Luckily for me, I was already a competent public speaker, so this was easy for me to do.

High school graduation photo, 1959

BASSWOOD LODGE AND RESORT

Toward the end of my high school years, sometime in May of 1959, I was told that I would be leaving the Rivards and going to work at a resort, Basswood Lodge on Long Lake near New Auburn, for the summer. It was located back in my home county. Miss Hartfiel had arranged this work for me because she thought it would be a good experience for me before going off to college in River Falls. It turned out to be a wonderful summer as I met many cultured, sophisticated, and professional people who helped me grow into someone more self-assured and away from the socially delayed teenager I was at that time.

Basswood Lodge was a resort located on the northeast shore of the lake, primarily for fishermen who came to pull fine specimens of walleye, bass, muskie, and other Wisconsin species out of Long Lake's pristine, beautiful water. Businessmen, medical doctors, and publishers also came, mainly from cities in Illinois, such as Rockford, Peoria, and Chicago, and brought their families year after year to this rustic and unspoiled area of Chippewa County northeast of the town of New Auburn.

George Wolf, who seemed ancient to me, was the owner of the lodge, and his daughter, Dolly, and her husband, Frank Csongedi, helped him run it during the summer months only. Dolly and Frank had one son whom they called Frankie, who was about a year younger than I and a little heavy as his mother was. Frankie was quiet and nice, and we often talked, swam, or worked together. Frank, who functioned as the all-around maintenance man, was gentle and quiet and always wore a light-colored cap.

Mr. Wolf arranged for me to get my Social Security card, and I was informed that I would earn fifty dollars a month, which I intended to use to get some clothes and supplies for college. I did receive a little extra occasionally, in tips from fishermen who asked me to iron their shirts in the evening hours after my obligations were finished for the day.

Miss Hartfiel must have made an agreement with Mr. Wolf, my employer, to drive me to six-thirty mass every Sunday in a church in Bloomer. This he did faithfully, never missing a Sunday, and always on time for the half-hour drive there. He waited patiently for me for nearly a full hour and got me back in time to help Dolly serve guests their breakfast.

The main building was large, brown, and plain, with a sun porch that ran the entire length of the west side of the lodge. A massive table occupied the whole space and was where we served the guests, sometimes up to twenty-five or more at a time.

A bar-lounge area, where I rarely went, faced the lake at the south side of the lodge, bordered by another porch with a swing on it, and there were some bedrooms on the first floor. Additional bedrooms for guests, mainly single, dedicated fishermen, were on the second floor. My room, which had very steep steps leading up to it, was on the third floor at the west end of the building, more like an attic space but adequate for me, in spite of its relentless heat. I don't remember any air conditioning anywhere in the lodge, and usually the evenings were cool and comfortable. Being an avid Elvis fan, I decorated the walls and sloping ceiling with photos of him along with photos of other singing or acting idols of the time, such as James Dean and Rock Hudson, and listened to my small radio given to me as a graduation present by my sister Gladie and her husband, Lenard.

Dolly's kitchen was located, handily, to the east of the porch, where she conjured up delightful meals three times a day for the guests who all were on the American plan while they stayed with us for a week or more at a time. Her food was always delicious and satisfying. The menu was varied; however, breakfast always alternated between eggs with bacon or sausage, toast or English muffins, and crêpes suzette. I loved when Dolly taught me how to make the crepes, but more importantly, she showed me how to place a serving fork into each crepe, roll it, and elegantly place it on a guest's plate with a final flourish.

Fridays were always meatless as many of the guests were Catholic and did not eat meat on that day. For dinner on those days, spaghetti with a plain but tasty tomato sauce was served or fish or a tuna entrée of some sort. No matter what Dolly made, it was delicious. Even though I had been cooking since I was ten and had taken home economics all four years of high school, she taught me many skills in cooking, which I use to this day.

The french cream cake that Dolly often served was a true gourmet's delight. Made entirely from scratch, it consisted of a yellow vanilla cake which she sliced in half horizontally, then filled the space between with a marvelously delicious crème pudding, also vanilla. She frosted this entire masterpiece with lightly-flavored, real whipped cream on all sides then chilled the cake until serving time. Cool and elegant, it was the perfect summertime dessert.

Along with the main lodge, the resort consisted of ten cabins or cottages that lined the edge of the lake. They were all named after famous hotels in Chicago, such as the Edgewater Beach, the Blackstone, the Drake, the Sherman, Cozy Cottage, Lone Pine, and "the four 'ishy' ones": The Linder, the Capitol, the Chateau, and one more I do not remember the name of. It was probably the cottage that Frankie used as I referred to one in my diary as "Frankie's cottage," which Dolly and I cleaned. I referred to them in my diary as the "ishy" ones because they were older than the others and not as nice. A comparable word nowadays would be *yucky* or *gross*.

Along the edge of the lake to the east of the dock was a fish-cleaning station that saw a lot of action as fishing was good on Long Lake. At the end of the pathway from the lodge to the lake was a set of white benches canopied by vines and flowers, shielding the people sitting there from the sun. We often sat there, enjoying the magnificent view across this wondrous lake.

Dolly with young guest, summer 1959;
Basswood Lodge in background

I cleaned every room and cabin each day as they were rarely vacant and almost always full. In addition, I did the cleaning and dusting, mopping, and ironing, and I helped with the laundry. We hung the sheets and other linens on clotheslines, and Dolly showed me how to "professionally" fold sheets so that they could just be unfolded onto the bed for easier bed making and didn't need ironing, except for the pillowcases. She also showed me how to make a bed as they do in hotels.

One of my other little jobs that I enjoyed was to go out by the clotheslines and snip fresh chives, which Dolly added to cottage cheese and some of her other dishes.

There was some time for fun too. Nearly every Saturday night, Frank and Dolly took me dancing at one of the many dance halls prevalent in Wisconsin at that time in Salisbury, Birch Point, the Pines, or Bruce. Frank and Dolly never left me alone, and I appreciated their watchful eyes, making sure I was always safe. These dance halls could get pretty rough at times as most of them had a bar at one end and alcohol made some of the dancers brave beyond what was acceptable. Some of these dance halls were divided, with people under age eighteen on one end and those older at the other end. In Wisconsin at that time, people could drink beer at age eighteen, with an ID, of course, which everyone wanted to get as soon as they could.

We went to movies too, all of us together as a group and sometimes with guests. I never went anywhere alone, not even shopping, a precaution against harm, I now know, that must have been agreed upon by Frank, Dolly, and Mr. Wolf with Miss Hartfiel. Having no car and no driver's license, I couldn't go on my own, anyway, and Basswood was too far from New Auburn or other town to go or walk there alone.

Being on the lake, of course we had to take advantage of the inviting water and swim. We sometimes swam as long as two hours in the afternoon and also at night, and many times the guests would join us. We often interacted with the guests as well when we played cards or sat around chatting. I learned to play the card game euchre, which continues to be one of my favorites. Many evenings, we heard laughing kids from across the lake who were at summer camp or having a party. These kids, I thought, were from wealthy families, very different from my own family. Now, of course, I know better; these kids came from "normal" families with hardworking parents.

Luckily for me, one of our families from Rockford had a Chris-Craft boat with which they could pull water-skiers. Their tall, dark, and handsome nineteen-year-old son, Ronnie, happily taught me to get up again and again until I could manage the skis and stay out of the way of the ropes, which could leave nasty burns on one's legs if held onto too long before falling. Waterskiing was big then, especially in the Wisconsin Dells where Tommy Bartlett's famous skiers put on shows in the summer for vacationers.

When it was time for me to leave Basswood Lodge and go to college, I cried as much when I left Dolly and Frank as I had cried when I left Richard and Mary at the beginning of the summer. Miss Hartfiel had been correct that the summer job there would be a good experience for me. My sister Ruby followed me there two years later; however, when she got to the lodge, Mr. Wolf was the only one there. Frank and Dolly had not yet arrived from their winter home in Stuart, Florida. Ruby told me that she was afraid there alone with Mr. Wolf and returned to Chester and Helen's. Too bad, as that would have been a fine experience for her too had she stayed. Maybe it was Mr. Wolf's name that scared her away, but he was a fine old gentleman.

OFF TO "COW COLLEGE"

In the spring of our senior year of high school, several of us were taken to visit the campus at River Falls, known then as Wisconsin State College at River Falls, located about thirty-five miles southwest of Glenwood and about half an hour southeast of Saint Paul. We were given a tour and treated to lunch in the cafeteria, which at that time was located in the lower level of South Hall. I never looked at or considered attending any other college, even though Mr. Page, my English teacher who directed our plays, had recommended Eau Claire because it had a better theater department (in his opinion, for he had not obviously met Dr. Davis).

With its green, rolling terrain, beautiful old North and South Halls, and being known for its friendly, knowledgeable staff, I remember thinking, *I can be happy here.* I never regretted that decision. My friends and classmates from Glenwood, Julie and Tom, also chose River Falls. Tom was a star athlete and participated in football and basketball while there, became a coach, teacher, and referee, and Julie became an elementary teacher. After fulfilling the requirement of hundreds of clinical hours in speech therapy and student teaching in the areas of speech and English at the high school level under the supervision of J. Henry Gingras in New Richmond, I graduated with a degree in secondary education. My major was in speech, with double emphases in theater and speech therapy (changed later to pathology) and a minor in English.

River Falls had the nickname "Cow College" (also "Bovine U", and "Moo U") because there was a large population of students studying agriculture in addition to having a highly rated program in education. With student enrollment at that time of about 2,500, the ratio of males to females was about three to one, with females benefitting from the unequal ratio. Wayne, who was one of the photographers for the *Student Voice* newspaper, talked me into modeling that inequity with three young men as a visual presentation of the lopsided ratio for one of the weekly paper's articles. Just recently, I attended my 50th Golden Jubilee Reunion on campus and learned that the ratio is now about 60 percent female and 40 percent male.

L to R: My roommates, Erma & Julie and friend, Judy

I learned that my roommates in Hathorn Hall ("Hag Hall"), the only women's dorm then, would be Julie and someone named Erma from Saint Croix Falls. We were crammed into room 106 at the front of the building, three to a room, two of us sleeping in bunk beds. Erma chose the top bunk because she was taller than I with nice long legs, and I had the lower because I was the shorty in the trio. We meshed together very well and enjoyed three years of being roommates until I moved into 125 South Third Street and had AnitaKay as my roommate. She shared her clothes, shoes, watch, and jewelry with me, so I was well-dressed during my student-teaching assignment. She spent time that winter hand knitting a pair of angora skating socks for me, which I still treasure.

Judy and Edie next door also spent time with us, and Judy was the guitarist and main harmonizer to our little singing (and yodeling) group, the Harmonettes, comprised of Judy, Julie, and me. Erma declined to join us. She willingly kept track of all of our purses while we were on stage; and one time, a policeman approached her to question her about why she had all of them. Luckily, he believed her true reason for being a "bag lady" before that term came into the lexicon. We won the Rutabaga Festival talent contest in Cumberland the year we entered and sang Johnny Cash's song "I Walk the Line" (very popular at that time) and the comedic "There's a Hole in the Bottom of the Sea."

Hathorn Hall's lower level was where we usually practiced and sang occasionally for all the residents. This was where we had the myriad meetings of a college dorm—too many in retrospect, I now think. There was a full kitchen and a lounge area where we could entertain, nearly always as a group, and where our friend Hussein taught us how to make Pakistani *kima*, which we made often. This dish was made with hamburger, potatoes, small green peas, and curry flavoring. No males were allowed anywhere else in the building. Even the janitor, a male, had to call down the hallway "Man on the floor" or "Man in the hall" to give a heads-up to young residents to be properly covered when he came there to clean.

In Hathorn Hall Lounge, Bev, friend Hussein
from Karachi, Pakistan, Erma

One night, my friends and I saw two of our friends, Tom and Larry (Porky) below our window. We sneaked them in somehow through a window and sat in our room talking and laughing for quite a long time. Luckily, we were not found out; however, someone not in on the shenanigans wondered aloud later upon seeing something quite odd: "I wonder how those footprints got on the ceiling!" I forgot this until many years later when all of us roommates met for one of our regular get-togethers and were discussing humorous incidents from that time.

There were two doors at the front of the building with vestibules to each side that we all called the Passion Pits, where young lovers bid each other good-night, lingering for lengthy periods. Nearly everyone, I think, had her turn there with a special friend. With the rigid rule about keeping punctilious hours, in retrospect I'm surprised that this was even allowed.

"THE ROAD TO HELL"

We had strict hours to observe in Hag Hall, and if there were infractions, one would be "campused," forced to stay in the hall, in one's room, with no visitors or phone calls during weekend nights and sometimes during the week too. Needless to say, that was detested, and today, young ladies would scoff at such clamping down and would flat out refuse to cooperate. We always had to be in the hall by ten thirty on weekday nights and by twelve on weekends, just like Cinderella. Nearly everyone was "campused" at one time or another, and it was aggravating. Miss Bowman, our faculty live-in resident advisor, must have grown weary of all of us young ladies being so wayward.

Larry, Bev, Mickey at Shady Grove

When I was "campused," which happened a number of times and one time at least for two weeks straight, my dancing partners, Mickey and Larry, were not happy. Larry and Mickey were very good friends, both extremely handsome and polite, and were from Knapp, a small town not far from Glenwood, so Julie and I often rode back and forth with them as neither of us had a vehicle. Mickey, according to my diary, "dances just like I do," and Larry, in addition to being an accomplished pianist, was the best at dancing the seductive tangos and other such dances where the man's leg goes in between the woman's thighs. Such dances gave rise to the statement that dancing is "a perpendicular expression of a horizontal desire" or "upper persuasion for lower invasion," as Karl, a student from Brazil, used to say. Decades later, the hit movie *Dirty Dancing* would feature this same type of dancing, though I never heard it called that when we danced. We maybe would have thought of it as *naughty* or *suggestive*, but certainly not *dirty* dancing. Larry and I danced in all the best ballrooms, including the Prom Ballroom in Saint Paul and the Aragon in Chicago, a most elegant venue, one time when I was in that city for a speech and hearing convention and Larry was there visiting relatives who lived on Central Ave.

The Aragon was the epitome of dance halls with its shiny bentwood floor that rested on a cushion of cork, felt, and springs, artificial stars twinkling overhead, and clouds projected to appear to float across the domed roof sixty feet above the dance floor. The entire dance hall was a replication of a Spanish palace courtyard, with its crystal chandeliers, mosaic tiles, and beautiful arches. Dancers in semiformal evening wear, which was always required, filled the dance floor the night we danced there. This night of dancing with such a breathtaking dance partner as Larry was truly a night of exquisite fantasy, comparable to Cinderella's dance with the prince. Sadly, Larry died at the age of thirty-nine, a young victim of cancer. He did have nights of magic, though, which I can say with certainty, because they were nights of enchantment for me too. I am sad for young people today who will never know such allurement because those elegant old dance halls and ballrooms no longer exist, and the culture has changed so drastically.

One night, I was quite late coming back and signing in because I was out with a good friend from my hometown, spending the time in quality conversation (and some smooching too, I admit). We lost track of time, and I paid for that infraction dearly.

I was called in to see the dean of women students. Dr. Knaak was a single, middle-aged lady doing her best to see that all of us babes in the woods remained pure and virtuous on her watch.

She asked me why I was so late; I told her that we lost track of time and that I had good intentions of getting in before the deadline. She pulled Rudyard Kipling's line on me, telling me that "the road to Hell is paved with good intentions," then suspended me for the rest of that week. As it was a Tuesday, that meant a lot of wasted days for me. I had to call Mary to tell her to come and get me. Thankfully, she did not nag or hassle me, and I regretted not being punctual getting back into "Hag Hall." Sometimes, though, a great conversation is worth the punishment. Can't beat a good talk session. To this day, having a quality conversation with a special friend or loved one is one of my all time favorite things to do.

There was a time that my grades were not up to my usual standards due to being so busy with rehearsals, productions, and work, and Miss Hartfiel asked me if maybe I should consider going into the two-year teaching program instead of the full four-year program. I was not interested in this, so I renewed my efforts to get my grades back up where they belonged. Thankfully, grades for my final course work during my last two years were nearly all As. Miss Hartfiel's kind, considerate talk with me put me back on track, and I reduced my theater involvement to concentrate more on my grades. Those grades helped me to obtain an assistantship for my graduate work.

"REMEMBER TO EAT YOUR PROTEIN!"

Because I had chosen the field of speech as my major from the very beginning, I had a number of classes with Dr. Blanche Davis ("Doc D" behind her back, but always her full title to her face). She was a lady to be reckoned with. Having earned her PhD from Columbia in New York, she was a firm taskmaster, a perfectionist, and a drill sergeant all rolled into one. She was dignity, elegance, and perfection personified. She would accept no excuses for not being prepared either in class or on the stage. Among all the other skills we learned, we had lessons in learning how to be more observant in order to become better actors and speakers. I use those observational skills even today and have shared them with others, including my sons and in my work with children.

Dr. Davis expected perfect diction, correct pronunciation, and full, rich volume, with the voice thrown to the back of the room for strong projection. She encouraged me to extinguish colloquialisms from my speech. Often, at first, she would comment on my comment/criticism sheet after one of my speeches, that I had said such words as *genuine*, *cigarette*, *extraordinary*, *because*, or *sword* incorrectly and that there were no such words as *gotta*, *git*, or *git goin'*. The word *yah* was not acceptable for *yes*, and *amina* was not accepted for "I'm going to," or *proly* or *probly* for *probably*. In addition, one of my classmates, Vince, who hailed from Cudahy south of Milwaukee, was often encouraged to get his speech up to her standards. *Dis*, *dat*, *deze*, *dem*, and *doze* were not accepted. If there had been any students from certain areas of Chicago, I presume she would have told them the same thing. We all emerged eventually as polished and eloquent speakers and presenters up to her demanding and high standards. There are a number of TV reporters/personalities who could have benefitted from being in Dr. Davis's classes.

As theater majors, we were all expected to learn the technical aspects as well as the performing and had to learn to build and paint flats for sets, paint scrims, learn the lighting board and how to operate it, take a course in directing, know the entire *History of the Theatre*, every playwright and his or her plays, learn makeup selection and application (even in the dark and without a mirror), everything about costuming, both making and selecting them. We also learned how to change an outfit in front of others without revealing anything, a handy technique to know. We were lucky to have had the help of Grandma Wonderly, Dr. Davis's mother, and many times we went to their home just north of the campus to work on costumes, especially the luxurious and elaborate Elizabethan gowns and capes with their high collars and heavy beading on the lush, weighty fabrics.

I participated in many of her exceptional productions, playing the roles of the white rabbit in *Alice In Wonderland*, the senile old grandmother in *The House of Bernarda Alba*, Mattie in our Readers' Theater production of *Ethan Frome*, a lady-in-waiting in *Taming of the Shrew*, and others; however, my favorite role was that of Ophelia in *Hamlet*, which I played on alternate nights as Dr. Davis had cast two of us in that role in order to give us both that opportunity.

When we weren't in a play, we were expected to help with the technical aspects of a production. When we were backstage, often our friends would call out among the costumes, flats, and sets, "Hey! Bev," and either both my friend Bev and I would answer or neither of us would. This was frustrating for our friends, so Dave, a mutual friend, decided that he would rename us Big Bev, my friend as she is five feet ten with the personality to match and Little Bev, because I was short, just five feet two, and basically quiet. Those names have stuck with us, and whenever we are both with mutual friends, they resort to those monikers. Even our sons use those terms when we are both present.

Dr. Davis was known for her unrelenting and uncompromising standards of quality, choosing to do Shakespeare, Garcia-Lorca, Melville, Moliere, and avant-garde plays by the existentialists, such as *No Exit*, *The Zoo Story*, *Under Milkwood*, and *Waiting for Godot*, and works by the brooding Irish playwrights rather than the fluff (her opinion) of musicals. She did *Tiger at the Gates* the year I was a freshman and told me that she strongly considered me for the prime role of Helen of Troy; however, even though I physically looked the part, my experience was far too lacking to play the vampy, alluring Helen. Dr. Davis told me that my voice wasn't "sexy enough," and she was right. Taloa, an intriguing brunette who did play Helen, did a fine job as the golden goddess from Troy.

Dr. Davis gave a standing order to all of us thespians, especially during the final weeks of rehearsal and production: "Don't forget to get your rest, and to eat your protein!" She knew way back then what to do to keep a body strong. We used a lot of energy during these busy weeks, and Dr. Davis did her best to keep us well.

We were all interested in being members of both Masquers and Alpha Psi Omega, and I was thrilled when I earned my pin for Alpha Psi. In addition to our work in The Little Theatre located at that time in the Chalmer-Davies Library, Dr. Davis took us to a number of professional productions in Minneapolis and Saint Paul. We were the children she did not have, and she fully expected us to come up to her high standards in every way. All of us in her program, many of us lost or broken young people, found ourselves and began to blossom in her rich, welcoming environment, coming out whole.

"MISS BOSINSKE, IF YOU WANT TO BE A TEACHER..."

All of my classes at River Falls were interesting, and there was a good variety to expose me to all areas of higher learning. There were many exceptional instructors and professors during my time there, including Francis P. Chisholm in English, Bennie Kettelkamp in biology, Robert "Doc" Bailey in sociology, Vera Moss in English, Drs. Berg and Darr in political science, Mr. Lewis, who taught Communications, Remedial Reading, and Structural Linguistics, among other classes (and who liked reminding us that we didn't *have* to be there in his class—the only two things we *had* to do were pay taxes and die). Dr. Anderson was known for walking across campus in the dead of winter with only a short-sleeved shirt and tie instead of a jacket or coat. The one who had the best name of all, Dr. Love, was a political-science professor.

Dr. Allan Siemers was the director of the secondary education program. One day he asked me to stay after class for a short time. His following words were another of the milestones on my path in life: "Miss Bosinske, if you want to be a teacher, you need to go and get that /r/ sound remediated." I knew that my /r/ sounds were said a little differently than most people said them as I learned how to talk from my older sister who talked the same way. We would say words with this sound as if we were from Boston, but as we were not, that was considered an error in speech production.

Dr. Siemers instructed me to go to the Speech Department on campus and to request an appointment for speech therapy as one could not become a teacher in Wisconsin with errors in speech production.

Teachers are role models for their students, including how they speak, so flawless articulation was a necessity. That is not always the case now as I have worked with several teachers with quite noticeable lisps or other speech errors. I used to cringe when I heard lower elementary teachers tell their students how to produce a specific sound when they said it incorrectly themselves.

I spoke with the only instructor in speech therapy at the time, William G. Larsen, and we set up therapy twice a week, Tuesday and Thursday afternoons, after my classes were finished for the day. This was all new to me; however, as it was another branch of speech, I found it quite fascinating. So interesting, in fact, that I soon decided that instead of trying to eventually get a job in theater, which may have required a tryout on a couch, I could actually make a living doing this type of speech work. I signed up for classes in this branch of speech and have been in this field ever since, to my great delight and satisfaction.

I progressed quickly through the stages of therapy and have ever since told my students that I fully understood that what I was asking them to do was hard as I could speak from personal experience. That was a great way to establish rapport and to gain their cooperation in this long, tedious, sometimes difficult remediation process.

Our speech therapy classes were always interesting and generally full. Our new speech instructor was excellent, with the same high standards of Dr. Davis or Dr. Chisholm who had hired the new instructor from Tucson, Arizona, on the basis of a phone call alone. I don't remember his first entrance to the classroom, but my friend Jerry told me many years later what his memory was of that initial entrance into his classroom. According to Jerry, he entered the room, wrote on the board "B. A. Larsen," which he said stood for "Bad Ass Larsen." That wasn't so, however, as the only thing he was "bad" about was his insistence on perfect spelling and flawless grammar in all our reports, tests, and clinical records. If there were any errors, the entire answer was marked wrong, so we all became expert spellers and grammarians, if we weren't already. It would be an unprofessional stain to incorrectly spell words in a report such as the ones we do in my field on a regular basis. To this day, I never misspell hemorrhage, diarrhea, or other such clinical terms. In addition, during my work years I was known for my excellent, informative, correct reports to parents and staff, delivered in a timely manner.

We were seated alphabetically then, so my classmate on my left was a twenty-year navy veteran who had been at Pearl Harbor on December

7, 1941, an English major who had four daughters. He would always nudge me with his elbow, then say, "Hey, doll, did you hear this one?" or "Did you hear the one about . . ." Bill could always be counted on to lighten the day with his off-color, sometimes downright raunchy jokes. He was part of the large contingent of veterans on campus known as the Vet's Club. I was saddened to learn that years later he suffered a stroke, the very thing those of us in speech and language fear because we understand how devastating and debilitating such an event can be.

Another of my classmates who went on to earn his PhD told me many years later that I always knew the answers to the questions on the tests because I was one of the few who had actually read the textbook. It's easy to learn and absorb information when it is interesting and significant, as information in my field most definitely is. As I recall, we were all good students who earned matching grades. No grades were given away freely back then and we all had to work for the As and Bs we wanted to see on our report cards. I don't remember any of us dropping out of this field of study or flunking out. The ratio of males to females at that time was about one to four as about 25 percent of students in the field were males. Now, there are very few men, maybe three percent, and most of them branch off into the area of audiology.

JOBS FOR SPENDING MONEY

One of my part-time jobs while I was at River Falls was in the library. I worked mainly in the reference books section located near the front of the library, so I was able to see and get to know nearly everyone on campus. I was paid sixty cents an hour, acceptable at that time, and I had wonderful, clean, safe working conditions, surrounded by all those books. Mrs. Belfiori, Jo's mother, was one of the librarians I worked with.

In addition to babysitting for extra money, I also worked as a waitress at Hansen's (one time O'Brien's) Cafe. This was also a great place to work. My friend Claudia helped me to get this job, which paid seventy-five cents an hour plus any tips we were given. Homemade food was the specialty, including the "Blue Plate Special" and homemade pies of all kinds. One of the employees had the job of only baking pies, commonly served in those days and enjoyed by everyone (before the days of guilt emerged).

One job that I often did was to iron blouses and other clothing for Edie, who lived next door in the dorm. I didn't mind this job, while she must never have done it in her life. She did look and dress like a girl who would be right at home at Vassar, and was the homecoming queen at the college in River Falls one year. There were other girls who looked and dressed like her also; however, I didn't consider myself one of them. I did observe and learn, though, so I could become more like them (proper and respected).

OUTSIDE THE CLASSROOM

Even though we spent a great deal of time on our classes and in Dr. Davis's productions, there was time for extracurricular activities. I participated in the synchronized swimmers, a group of young ladies who performed swimming skills set to music. I was a member of the Fathom Falcons and learned to scuba dive with friends from the Lake Geneva and Baraboo areas and also participated in political groups, Newman Center activities, and public discussion groups.

Quite a few evenings were spent at Shady Grove near Beldenville or Shady Rest (in Wilson, on our way home) as we could legally drink a beer or two or more at the age of eighteen. We liked the Little Joe beer by Schlitz that came in seven-ounce bottles or the fresh, delicious draft beer. The main reason for going to those places, though, was to meet others and to engage in conversation and frivolity and to dance. We always went in groups, and we looked out for each other's safety. Nobody had to worry about date rape at that time, either. At least I never heard of that happening back then.

These times at Shady's were sharply contrasted with the most genteel and elegant of teas, which were held quite often and with all the formality and beauty associated with this tradition. Sometimes, the teas were held at the private home of President and Mrs. Kleinpell, which was a special treat indeed. Such lofty times. My, my. This was living the way I liked. We did learn proper dress, etiquette, and manners, which served us well as we went through life. Now, tea parties seem to have survived only among young princesses or granddaughters and their grandmothers. My granddaughter and I often share a tea party with a little ceramic Disney Princess tea set that we keep in my home. It's never too early to begin to cultivate elegant manners and proper, thoughtful behavior and to develop good communication skills.

Most young men had their own cars, those big old "land yachts" crafted and authentic in the most minute detail. They had swept-back rear ends, fins that proclaimed which brand they were, large, impressive grills that announced their arrival, real leather interiors, including hand-stitched leather around the steering wheel (sometimes with a necker's knob on it), long bench seats, and no seat belts. It's a wonder we didn't all get killed riding around as we did and driving often after drinking beer. I remember driving Julie's car back to the dorm one time from Shady Grove when none of us in the car ought to have been behind the wheel. I was the one determined to be the least impaired, so I carefully paid attention, drove at a reasonable speed, and was glad when we arrived back at Hag Hall.

I dated a young man a few times who called himself Tex, and he lived up to that nickname. He was tall, brash, and supremely confident. He walked with languid ease and draped himself over furniture with abandon as if he were a part of it. He owned a brand new, bright-red Cadillac convertible with white leather interior and drove through town or campus like a rooster staking out his territory. Some young men, in contrast to Tex, drove older cars that they kept running themselves as is common in the state of Wisconsin. Those young men could fix anything.

During the last month or so of school, the most glorious time of the year in northwest Wisconsin, at least one night a week was spent at Clifton Hollow, a wooded spot sweeping down along County Highway F at the Kinnickinnic River's edge. With everything new and lush, celebrating the end of the long, frigid winter and a demanding school year was a real pleasure party. A keg or more of beer was brought out, tapped, and fully enjoyed by all who had come to celebrate as if this were a Bacchanalian festival. There was only drinking and singing, though, no sex that I ever saw, although some people may have sneaked away into the woods or into those roomy backseats. None of my business.

We often rode, all piled in, out to the Hollow with Jerry in his 1959 white Chevy Impala with the swept-back trunk like a swallow's tail. This was a gorgeous car, brand spanking new, with red interior. Jerry had no trouble getting dates as he came from a leading family in Lake Geneva and had impeccable manners, but the car certainly didn't hurt his chances. We always went in groups, and I never once heard of any problem happening for anyone during these parties. Maybe a few of us being "campused" once in a while, though, for coming in late.

There is a state park and golf course in the Clifton Hollow area now, so I presume that it is no longer used for the gatherings so popular half a century ago. The only gatherings there now are the elegant wedding receptions looking over the same beautiful green expanses we feasted our eyes and souls on so long ago. I don't think that this color green exists anywhere else on earth besides my beloved northwest Wisconsin. Or maybe it just seems that way because of all the promise such a new, fresh color invokes.

In the summertime most of us went swimming quite often in the Saint Croix River between Hudson and Prescott. We took picnics and beach gear for use out on the numerous sand bars that appeared at times when the water level was low enough to get to them. It was like having ones' own private island for relaxing and being away from it all.

Nearly everyone smoked cigarettes at that time, thinking the behavior to be sensual and glamorous, prompted by all the advertising that told us that. It was the height of sexiness for a young man to light a young lady's cigarette while she supported his hand, both of them gazing into each other's eyes with promise, at the very least, so if someone did not smoke, he or she was a target for pressure to suck them into the habit. Major tobacco companies gave away many boxes of samples, four cigarettes to each tiny pack, to entice new smokers. I remember that we all wanted to get these small boxes given away at the student union or in the dorms to try to lure others into joining us in our bad habit. Erma, who didn't smoke at all, was the last of our group to try to see what all the fuss was about. She didn't smoke very long, as I recall. I smoked almost six years, giving up the habit cold turkey the spring before I was married. By then, the evidence was overwhelming that this was a habit that was best to quit. I used the money I would have burned up and had my hair done each week when I was working full time, which was a much better use of the money than blowing it up in smoke.

College graduation formal drape shot, common at that time.
Photo by Gene Brown, Gene Brown Studios, River Falls, Wi.

JACK AND JACKIE
(Yes, Those Very Ones)

Late fall of 1959 and the early part of 1960 was an extremely busy time politically in the area of northwestern Wisconsin. River Falls, being only about a thirty-minute drive from the metropolitan area of "The Cities" of Minneapolis and Saint Paul, was a hotbed of activity, mainly because the chief opponent, during the primaries, of Senator John F. Kennedy was Hubert V. Humphrey who hailed from the state of Minnesota.

College campuses are notoriously famous for being politically active, and River Falls was no different. It was exciting to be involved in all the action, and there was an underrunning current of knowing that something really big was on the horizon about to happen.

At that time, I was a member of the Young Democrats because Richard and Mary were very active in that political party, and of course, it was obvious that this was the group of people who had the handsome, gregarious candidate in John F. Kennedy. Humphrey, being older and partially balding and a little heavy, though outgoing too, was not considered the candidate who could lead into the next exciting period of history by us students who supported Kennedy and worked diligently on his behalf.

Some of us were very lucky to be hostesses at various events such as "coffees" and other meetings to garner support for our candidate. We were fierce in that devotion to the cause. We also went door-to-door, ringing doorbells and passing out leaflets and flyers, always with the picture of the handsome, youthful candidate on the front. We had no idea at the time of JFK's personal predilections, and I doubt that his private behavior would have made any difference to the young people who supported him.

My roommate and friend Julie, also from Glenwood City, and I were given the honor of appearing at various events as "Miss Saint Croix County Democrat" (Julie) and "Miss Pierce County Democrat" (I). We were selected, with no competition, by the main Democratic Party, primarily Richard and his friends, I believe. We wore lovely cocktail dresses, the height of fashion at that time. Julie dressed in red lace and I in blue chiffon, with white satin banners proclaiming who we were in sparkly gold lettering. Julie, a stunning brunette being five feet ten inches, was elegant, and her full-throated laugh and liquid voice as she mingled among the crowd was delightful. I did my best to appear poised also, and the banner helped me to see myself as someone who wasn't too hard on the eyes. Thankfully, Dr. Davis's speech and public address training was helping me to appear more sophisticated and self-assured.

Jackie, ordinarily not present, was with Jack at one of the rallies, and I was able to shake her hand. She was extremely thin and delicate as she stood in the receiving line, welcoming those who had braved the winter weather to support her husband in his quest. Dressed in her classic, sleeveless, light-colored sheath, she wore elbow-length white kid gloves. The glove on her right hand showed considerable marks or dark color from having shaken so many hands of her and her husband's adoring public. Her hair was elegantly coiffed, makeup was flawless, and her guarded presentation of herself was cool, dramatic, and a little distant. I suppose, perhaps, because we rural Midwesterners were so different from her circle of friends and acquaintances. After all, Miss Porter's School, Vassar, and the Sorbonne, are not the same level as River Falls!

When the primary election was over, we continued to work in the general election, with the same happy outcome for our candidate. Thank-you letters came to some of us from the White House on official stationery, done with a typewriter, as computers had not yet been introduced to the masses for their use. Each letter was signed by our new president, a token of his appreciation for our help.

I still have all my Kennedy memorabilia, including buttons, newspaper articles, and three of his autographs. To my consternation, I do not have a copy of the picture that was in the River Falls Journal of Kennedy shaking my hand. The wording underneath said: "Freshman Beverly Bosinske of Glenwood City shakes the hand of Senator John F.

Kennedy on the lawn of North Hall." My long hair, flowing down my shoulders, was also included in the photo, and I was wearing the black coat with the red trim that I had brought with me from Cadott the day I was taken out of my home.

In my 1959 diary, on the date of November 12, which was a Thursday, I noted the following: "Kennedy came to give his speech. He was terrific! Such a good speaker and so handsome. I got his autograph twice, shook his hand once, and talked to him three times. There really were a lot of people there. I had my picture on TV tonight. I didn't see it; but other people told me they saw it. I was so impressed by Kennedy."

A few days later, on Monday, November 16, I wrote this: "My picture is in The Student Voice in two places this week—am I ever lucky! One is with Senator Kennedy. I'll really like to keep that one." I have often wished that I had a copy of that photo too. I have just one photo that I took of him with my old Brownie camera as he stood in the hall outside the auditorium of North Hall just after his inspiring speech to us that day. I asked if it would be all right to take his photo, and he immediately responded "Certainly" with the full Kennedy smile while holding his hands in front of him.

During my years of a stay-at-home mother and later while working in my professional shoes, I often presented a lesson for fifth graders who were studying the political system, and they were always amazed that here was someone with them who actually lived a part of history. I told them that President Kennedy was more handsome in real life than in his photos and had a charisma that is a rare beauty when seen.

Just a few years later, when I heard the unbelievable news about our young president's assassination, I was in my graduate program at NIU. I was about to leave my room just across from the Speech and Hearing Clinic to teach a one o'clock class when my roommate Donna told me what had happened. Everyone sat around crying at the senseless loss of one so young, vibrant, and full of promise, and the political world would never be the same. Walking to Newman Center just a short distance away and going to mass to say prayers in unison was the only thing we could think of to deal with this horrible tragedy. The weekend was a loss to anything productive for all of us.

For those of us who had actually met the president, worked on his behalf, and been in his glowing presence, it was a devastating blow, and all the hope and promise that was Camelot was no more.

During this time period, the only other famous person I met was Conway Twitty. He was thin and handsome then, looking very much like the young Elvis. My friends Erma, Julie, and Claudia, and I went to Ellsworth to attend his concert and met him and his band at the end. We also got his autograph, and I have several old black-and-white photos that I took with my faithful old Brownie camera.

STEAMBOAT INN, COFFEE CUP CAFE, AND RIVER FALLS NURSING HOME

During the summer of 1963, after having graduated from River Falls, I stayed in that town before going on to DeKalb, Illinois, and graduate work at Northern Illinois University. I had been awarded a teaching graduate assistantship through the DVR, the Division of Vocational Rehabilitation. There would be five of us assistants under Dr. Alpiner, working twenty hours each in the Speech and Hearing Clinic doing hearing evaluations, hearing aid evaluations, clinical observations and therapy, and teaching classes to deaf, hard of hearing, or severely speech-handicapped young adults in auditory training, lip (now called speech) reading, and speech/voice improvement. In addition to our work commitments, we would be carrying several graduate level courses each semester in Speech Pathology and Audiology as our program was called then. Now, our field goes by the title Communicative Disorders, and the two areas are separated out into Audiology and Speech Pathology.

It's hard to get a job just for the summer that pays any substantial amount, so I cobbled together three jobs to make ends meet. My job at the nursing home was as a nurse's aide doing all the hard work of bathing and feeding people who were unable to do those things themselves, helping with the bedpans, changing adult diapers for those who needed them, changing beds, and emptying catheter bags. The hardest job of all, however, was helping to give enemas to people who needed that procedure every few days. Actually digging impacted feces (gloved hands, of course) out of their colons was hard work, and believe me, that was humbling. I felt sorry for the old people who often cried out, "No, no, please. No, just let me die."

I loved those old people, and they let me know by the wide smiles on their faces when I arrived for work each morning that they were happy to see me. I had the early shift, from 7:00 a.m. until 3:00 p.m. On Sundays, I had to be up early to walk way across town from where I lived on Vine Street, south and west of the University, to St. Bridget's Church at the north side of town for the five-thirty mass. Then, the long walk back even farther to the nursing home located at the south edge of town at that time.

I remember talking with and caring for some of the patients as if it were today. Not having known them in their prime of life, I had no past memories to contend with. Seeing someone old and debilitated doesn't fit in with one's memory of that person young, vigorous, and lively, but I did not have any youthful memories to deal with and could appreciate these people now for what remained.

There was perpetually happy Mac, one of my favorite patients who had suffered a stroke, always doing his arm exercises in his doorway while reading the very tiny print of the financial columns. Mrs. Murphy, who was dying from breast cancer that had already eaten away all the top layers of her chest, lived there with her brother, who was a comfort to her. Lyle, who was forever sad, was destined to spend the rest of his days confined to a wheelchair because of an accident and whose catheter bag I had to change or empty every time I worked. I cared for a really big lady close to three hundred pounds whose name I don't remember. She had had one arm amputated, which made it even more difficult to help her in and out of the bathtub, as small as I was. There were no special tubs to use which open at the side, as they do now, for easy access.

Then there was the tiny lady withered away by Parkinson's disease and who let me know that she appreciated my help each time she took food by her sad and wistful look that tracked my movements. Her arms and legs had already become frozen into the fetal position, common with the progression of this disease, and she could no longer speak. She especially liked the softboiled eggs that were on the breakfast menu often. I would rap the smaller end with a firm whack of a knife then deftly scoop the egg out, which puddled in all its golden glory on the plate. She could easily swallow the soft eggs and liked them, which was gratifying.

Lastly, there was eighty-eight or eighty-nine-year-old Tom Quinn—tall, strong, and still physically imposing, with a full head of thick pure-white hair but, incongruently, with a strongly intact libido that was about eighteen years old. He would eye me lasciviously from across the room as I made his bed, cocking his head a little and moving his chin up and down a few times, then saying, "Unbutton that front," referring to the buttons of the bodice of my white uniform.

Not wanting to set him off or anger him, I would humor him by saying, "What for?"

Then he'd say, "I wanna see."

"There's nothing there to see," I would counter.

"I wanna see, anyway!" he would say.

Luckily, most of the time, that was all he would say or do. One time, however, he sneaked up behind me, put his arms around my waist, and hugged me—trying to relive his younger days, I suppose. Sad, for such a one-time Romeo.

This summer job at the nursing home was good experience for me when I got to the point in my graduate work of doing my hospital practicum. Some of the other grad students and I went every Thursday for about a year and a half to Schwab Rehabilitation Hospital, located at Twenty-Sixth and California in Chicago, just across the street from the infamous Cook County Jail. As student clinicians, we didn't wear lab or white coats, though the speech pathologists on staff and other professionals all did wear the universally recognized health-care garments. Being in a hospital was much different from the educational settings we had previously been in, except for one of us who had already worked at Johns Hopkins Hospital when she lived in Maryland.

I was glad that Dr. Williams—a big, humor-filled man, even though he was plagued with severe dysfluency—nearly always drove us there. Sometimes, Ira, a new student among us, would drive us there in his Volkswagen bug. I was glad when those rides (extremely cold, noisy, and uncomfortable) were over. Many years later, when my son Brian was director of the Research and Electronics Lab of Volkswagen of America in Palo Alto, California, I told him this story. By that time, however, there had been significant improvements to "the people's car."

The patients we served at Schwab Rehab Hospital were mainly older people who had suffered strokes and now showed symptoms of aphasia. We saw all types, of course: receptive, expressive, and global. It was sad to see them struggling to communicate, something they had done with ease and fluency when they were young. Now, there was sadness in their eyes. We worked with these people in groups or individually, gaining clinical hours and a wealth of information about this area of our field while doing the best we could to help them regain some semblance of normalcy in communicating. Sometimes, we had young people on our caseload, those who had been victims of car or motorcycle crashes, usually in their twenties. My saddest case was a young boy, about eight years old, who lived in one of the buildings of the projects of Chicago. He was standing outside, probably minding his own business, when someone high above dropped or threw a pop bottle out the window. Naturally, it landed squarely on his head, causing irreparable and traumatic brain injury.

My second job in the summer of '63 was just part-time and kitty-corner from 115 Vine where I lived with Earl and Minnie and my two roommates, Big Bev and Alice, another speech pathology student. I worked as a waitress, as I had at O'Brien's, then Hansen's Cafe, downtown River Falls. The Coffee Cup was a very small business in a very small space, but it was pleasant working there.

Another job I had that summer was in Prescott, a town about thirteen miles southwest of River Falls and along the beautiful Saint Croix River, filled with boats of all sorts and partying vacationers.

The Steamboat Inn was popular at that time and very busy, especially during the weekends. The restaurant had two levels with food and beverages: upstairs and the lower level, even with the ground, with expansive windows all across the west side, the better to view the gorgeous summertime sunsets above the water. I usually worked in the lower level that had a long bar at the east side of the room and was always busy. I worked as a barmaid taking drink orders and serving them to the customers. I don't remember how I learned about this job or arranged to get it.

I did not have to buy a special uniform but could wear what I chose, which in those days, was something that fully covered me but was attractive, even flirty. Young women, even those who worked in bars and restaurants were always discretely covered, in strong contrast to today, but we still liked to look our best.

My favorite outfit was one I purchased at Lynne-Rose, one of the ladies' stores in River Falls that always had fine and affordable garments. The two-piece set was in coral-colored cotton, my favorite color. The sleeveless top was bound at the jewel neckline by a white eyelet ruffle that was embroidered in coral thread and buttoned in back. The bottom, the eye-catcher of the set, was composed of two full skirts, the top one split entirely up both sides and bound with the same ruffle as the top. People often complimented me on my outfit, and I enjoyed wearing it. I sometimes wish I still had it.

Having no car (still), the owner would come to pick me up and then return me at the end of the evening's work. I don't remember his name, but he was always fair with me and never indicated to me that he had a problem coming to get me and taking me back home. Once in a while I would be offered a ride back to River Falls by a friend or customer.

The owner and others at Steamboat liked my work and the easy, friendly way I dealt with the customers. I think that I was a good asset to the business. I was sorry when I had to leave at the end of the summer. I never got back to Prescott again until many years later when Richard and Mary had a houseboat docked there and we took our sons to swim in the beautiful water of the Saint Croix River, to relax on the houseboat, and to picnic on the beach or one of the sandbars.

Toward the end of this summer, I received a letter from my mother, telling me that she had spent the last month crying her eyes out. Gladie's only son among three sisters, Little George or Junior, had drowned in Michigan. Evidently, he was with his biological father (Crazy George), and someone wasn't watching him. He was seven years old. Gladie never got over this loss (as all parents, I now know). Sad as this was, her heartache wasn't over, for three summers later, she would lose the love of her life, Lenard, her second husband, also in a drowning incident. As familiar as he was around water and as good a swimmer as he was, something seemed very odd to many of us about this entire situation. Lenard Jerome was as fine a man as one would ever want to know, a shirttail relative of Jennie Jerome, Winston Churchill's mother. Lenard had the same regal bearing as Churchill and was as different from Gladie's first husband as night is from day. Even though he had only one daughter with Gladie, he treated all four of her children as if they were his own, even dividing candy bars and other treats equally among them all.

Bev with Gladie's children Chetek High School May 1961.

Bev and Lenard, Ruby's graduation May 1961.

Ruby's Graduation May 1961.

Part III: Life in Illinois

"HEADS, IT'S COFFEE, TAILS, IT'S . . ."

Before moving to DeKalb, Illinois, to do my graduate work, I had gone there once before to meet with Dr. Alpiner, the director of my program, and to locate a place to live. On that first trip, my dear friend David, a gentle artist and one of the group of Lake Geneva young men attending River Falls, was kind enough to accompany me, driving us there in his little old red MG convertible sports car, which was really "living it up" in those days.

We didn't go straight into Illinois as David first took me home to meet his parents. His father was a mild-mannered barber with a little shop right downtown, close to the gorgeous and exclusive Lake Geneva, and his mother was a homemaker. Both were as kind and welcoming as their son and graciously made me feel right at home with them.

We had ridden back to Lake Geneva with other friends from that town because the MG had been in David's parents' garage up on blocks during the time David had spent in France before coming to River Falls. After getting home, he got it down off the blocks then up and running. Those old classic cars can always be relied on to perform for their owners.

In the afternoon the next day, we drove around the south shore of the lake, warm sun and cool breezes kissing our faces while we took in the beauty that is Lake Geneva. David had given me a lovely long lavender chiffon scarf to wrap my hair, which I kept for many years, until it was no longer presentable to wear in public. I have also kept the memories of those very special days as they can never be replaced or replayed.

The evening in Lake Geneva was as special as the afternoon had been. We had several friends who lived on the west side of the lake, in the exclusive area near the Wrigley Estate. We walked along that part of the lake before going across the lake by speedboat with friends Jerry and Howie to the pavilion area near downtown. This is a special building with businesses catering to vacationers, such as boat tickets for a sight-seeing ride around the lake, homemade candies, popcorn, souvenirs, T-shirts, and other such items. We also danced there and enjoyed being near the lake to observe the activity of sailboats and speedboats. This was a carnival atmosphere that played to the young and the young at heart. I could not have been any happier if I had been on the French Riviera or in Monte Carlo. This was living!

After leaving the pavilion, we went to an older establishment west of the town of Lake Geneva on Highway 50 going toward Lake Como, named Grandma Vitkus' Rustic Inn. The name was a good match as the building was run-down and brown, but we didn't care. It was fine for socializing. The owner, an older lady, was at a card table at the back, observing the goings-on in her establishment. She would take a shot glass with ice cubes from a tray, add liquor, then grab a bottle of soda or whatever was handy to add to her drink. Her granddaughter served the drinks while Grandma supervised her business. All my friends whom I knew from River Falls were there celebrating and enjoying life. This building stood for decades, and I checked it out when we took our sons to this area when they were little. Eventually, it was no more—just a memory for some of us on the now-vacant land.

As David and I drove into the state of Illinois the next morning, both of us noticed and commented on the deplorable condition of the roads compared to those we drove on in Wisconsin. The iconic Highway 38 (part of Route 66) especially, which led into DeKalb from the east, was like a washboard. As we drove into DeKalb, I thought, *I wonder when we will get to the "good" part of town.* Well, DeKalb was not very large then, and before we knew it, we were already in the midst of NIU, and there was not much more to the city of DeKalb. That was OK with me, though, as I am not a fan of big cities, preferring those that I can easily manage and navigate through.

After my meeting with Dr. Alpiner and, with his help locating a room on Lucinda Ave. right across from the Speech and Hearing Clinic, David drove me into O'Hare International Airport in Chicago for my flight back to Minneapolis and then to Wisconsin. I flew out because my former roommate, theater participant, and very good friend Big Bev was in labor and about to deliver her son, Guy, who is my godson.

Bev and Godson, Guy

That first flight was awesome. We flew into the sunset, which was as lovely as all the travel brochures depicted, gradually fading into the night and etched forever into my long-term memory. Back then, there was room to move and stretch, great food, excellent service, and no embarrassing search lines to endure. It would be nice if every flight for every passenger could be like that first flight was for me on August 21, 1963.

Another mode of travel that has nearly gone by the way in this country is elegant train travel. I had the pleasure of traveling by rail often on my trips back and forth between DeKalb and northern Wisconsin. The ride along the Mississippi River was beautiful, relaxing, and affordable. I traveled between Rochelle, Illinois, and Saint Paul, Minnesota, which took about eight hours and was a wonderful respite from my busy pace.

When I went back to DeKalb in early September to begin my commitment there, an acquaintance from River Falls, Dee, offered to drive me as she was going back to Chicago to work there. I knew who she was and had talked with her a few times but did not know her well. She was in the class just ahead of me and we never had any classes together. She had been an active leader, however, in various clubs on campus.

It was **an eight-hour drive at that** time between River Falls and DeKalb because the interstate had not yet been completed in the central portion of Wisconsin. We got into DeKalb after the dinner hour and unloaded my luggage. Dee said, "Let's go get some coffee downtown." I agreed, and we drove down to the main area of DeKalb. After searching for some place to get coffee and having no luck at all, Dee said, "Tell you what—" Then, taking a coin out of her back pocket, she finished her proposal, "Heads, it's coffee. Tails, it's booze."

That sounded fine to me as we were most likely not going to find any place that was still open that served coffee anyway. The coin landed on Dee's hand as tails up, so no coffee.

We walked about two blocks when Dee spied an establishment proclaiming in big silver letters: Andy's. She said, "This looks like a 'Johnny's' type of place." Johnny's was a bar in River Falls that the older students went to, including Dee, and I knew about but had only been in there a time or two.

Outgoing and handsome, with a full head of beautiful black waves and warm brown eyes, the man behind the bar looked like the model he had, a short time ago, been. Dressed in dark slacks and a short-sleeved white oxford dress shirt, he was the model of efficiency and service.

Above: The sport jacket is in a faint overcheck, in shetland and in wool; ~55. Vest is all wool; ~0. At Finchley's.

Good Mixers: Sport Coats With Olive

The popular plaid design in summer sport coats, this one in a combination wool and Polyester fabric. By Fashion Park. $65 at Finchley.

The natural shoulder suit, shown here with a vest, is basic. This is an imported worsted, $85 at Finchley.

Finchley Men's Wear, a fine establishment on Jackson Boulevard in Chicago's Loop and well-known for their traditional natural-shoulder clothing, had lost their lease in the summer of 1963, so they went out of business. After six years of working there and doing all the modeling for Finchley for newspaper and magazine ads, this young man in his mid-twenties was back at home temporarily before deciding what to do with the rest of his life. He had already served in the military with his two-year stint in the navy as a disbursing clerk, having been on an aircraft carrier and a submarine in the Caribbean, including Cuba, as that was before Castro came into power.

With a ready hand extended to greet us, Gene Finn introduced himself, and thus it was: I have forever after told people (including our sons) that I met Gene on a flip of a coin because there were no places open that served coffee on that night of destiny.

Mike, the owner of Andy's, came into the bar during our conversation and hired me on the spot as a barmaid after he learned that I had done that work in the summer. He had some very busy nights, especially Wednesday, as that was car auction night, which meant big spenders and big drinkers. I worked two or three nights a week to supplement my $220 a month from my assistantship. I never had to worry about being hassled by tipsy customers as, early on, Gene and I began dating. Once in a while, customers would take my left hand, examine it, and state something like this: "Why no ring?" or "What's a pretty little thing like you doing with no ring?" or "Why aren't you married?" When I told them that I was studying Speech Pathology and Audiology at the graduate level, they understood then that that pursuit was important too. I loved seeing the looks on people's faces when I told them about my field.

After this night with Dee, I never saw or communicated with her again. I learned a number of years later that she had committed suicide. She never got over her childhood ordeal of her father's abuse, another example of a ruined childhood and a ruined life.

My two years of graduate work went fast, and I continued to enjoy my chosen field. During this two-year period, Gene and I continued to be with each other, and we talked about the future, especially Gene's, as I already knew which path I was on. With many openings for speech pathologists, I would have no trouble getting a job. I couldn't wait to be in a respectable position. We talked about marriage, and I told Gene that I would not marry him as a bartender as he had more potential than that. And he could forget about going out to Las Vegas and working as a dealer. That was not going to work at all as far as I was concerned, and I would have none of that.

I asked him about what he would really like to do, and he said that he had always wanted his own store. I told him that he should try that. I had faith in his abilities and knowledge about fine menswear, and I would support him in that endeavor. He saved about $5,000 and looked into a location, getting goods, and figuring out all the other details of being an entrepreneur. The business was officially started when Gene opened a business account at the bank where his dad, a self-employed heating contractor, was a longtime customer. Gene was very happy when the bank agreed to open a small line of credit for him. In those days, every manufacturer asked for a bank reference and a contact person for a small start-up business. In addition, businesses were rated by Dun & Bradstreet, a company that maintains information on businesses and corporations for use in credit decisions.

One source of funds for Gene's future business was from the football parlay cards that he would distribute to the customers in Andy's. One of Gene's brothers and his friend were into this form of sports betting, distributing many cards to all kinds of businesses, especially taverns and restaurants. Parlay cards attracted handicappers, people who were die-hard college football fans. People would place their bets of one to five dollars on college football games that were played all over the country every week. There was a point spread that the Vegas oddsmakers set up. The lottery was not in play at this time, so this was one way that those with a penchant for gambling on their favorite teams could get their thrills for a small amount of money (or learn to deal with disappointment).

I was usually the "bag lady" for taking all that cash to the bookie in Aurora, at the southeast edge of town, to a bar called the Railroad Inn located along the railroad tracks in an area that looked and smelled like skid row. Maybe it was. How I ever did that, I don't know as now I would not even venture anywhere near a place like that. The room at the back was just as you would picture it: heavy smoke permeating and hanging over everything, hunched and disheveled men tending to figures and piles of cards and cash, and a pervasive edginess to it all.

The money was counted, the parlay cards taken and placed in stacks, and Gene's (and his brother's) cut of the earnings in addition to the money owed the betters, stuffed back into the bag. I was always glad when I could get out of there, into the light and the fresh air, and on my way back to DeKalb. I don't like to think of the bad kinds of things that could have happened on one of those money runs, but I was lucky, once again, and stayed safe and unharmed. I was glad that I went there Saturday mornings, in broad daylight, and not at night.

Along with money Gene saved from his job of tending bar, this extra money (even though it was certainly "earned") went into his stash, which gradually grew until he thought it would be enough to bring his dream to fruition. He located a workable space, shaped like a slice of pie, just east of the railroad tracks that ran through the center of town. Plans were made to open his very own store at 505 East Lincoln Highway on September 1, 1965, just eleven days after our wedding.

Finn's Ltd. was an instant success, and Gene worked hard, long hours on his own to make it so. I helped out occasionally on the weekends or after I came home from my job. I supported us for the first four years, and all Gene's profit went back into the business to build it.

Gene and I decided to get married in August, after my summer session would be over and before my new job would begin. We chose August 21, and low-key plans were made. There was no money for an engagement ring, and that was all right with me. I could forgo having a sparkling ring on my finger for a long-term dream. I could always get a ring later if I really decided that I wanted one. We didn't have much money to spend on our wedding, so I asked Grace Rhodes, a seamstress who did alterations and made ensembles for me, for her help. She made my dress that I designed and also my three attendants', Big Bev and my sisters Ruby and Michelle, from patterns she created. She charged me a pittance I think because she never had a daughter, just two sons. The entire cost of the dresses and headpieces, including fabric and her magic, was about twenty-five dollars. Grace was very good to me; she matched her name perfectly. Mr. Malone, the owner of a fine department store in DeKalb and already quite old, was kind enough to drive personally into Chicago to purchase the satin, silk organza, and french alençon lace I wanted because they weren't available in his own store. That kind of service is unheard of nowadays.

Gene & Bev in first apartment (Finn Apartments), DeKalb, Il. Fall, 1965

We sought Fr. Niggemann's consent to have Richard's brother, Fr. John, the priest serving Somerset, say the Nuptial High Mass and marry us. Fr. John, much like his brother, was genial and outgoing with a wonderful sense of humor and an uplifting laugh. His sermon for us was one that should be a model for others, but back then, people did not record major events in a lifetime for posterity. I often wish that I could go back and listen to it again. One of my favorite memories of Fr. John had been captured in a photo video. He was walking around the lawn in Glenwood, dressed in appropriate garments, saying his Divine Office (prayers said every day by priests). Fr. John was reverently walking, reciting his prayers, followed by all seven of Richard and Mary's children, and I believe they were in birth order, from oldest to youngest. Priceless.

For three weeks before our wedding day, the weather was perfect in Glenwood, and for two weeks after. On the twenty-first, however, it rained all day until about six o'clock. We had planned an outdoor reception on the expansive lawn, but that was not to be. We made the best of it, dancing and enjoying ourselves all over the house, including the basement. Some say that if it rains on your wedding day, you will have a prosperous life together. I think that is said to make people feel better.

Mary had made petit fours, we had sandwiches and other light foods, and a small white wedding cake with a hand-beaded topper that Mary had created that was the Catholic symbol for marriage, a cross with two circles entwined, circled by another round of beads. Fresh flowers were our decorations along with our bouquets of cymbidium orchids and spider mums and, for my bouquet, a gorgeous, fringed white orchid that could be removed from the center for wearing on our "going-away trip." I had wanted roses, but in a small town like Glenwood, one cannot always get what one wants. We were happy with what was sent and appreciated what everyone had done to make our day special.

We went to dinner with out-of-town friends and some family members at the Coachman, a restaurant in Baldwin, and returned to Glenwood. By this time, the weather was lovely and warm. We stayed until about ten then I changed into the obligatory "going-away outfit," which Grace had also made for me. It was a beige two-piece suit with pencil skirt, a jacket with a small portrait collar, three large bone buttons down the front, and small vents at the front of the hip bones. Elbow-length sleeves were met by the ever-present gloves, beige this time, and I wore a sleeveless coral satin shell underneath made from leftover fabric of my attendant's dresses. The orchid center of my bouquet was on my left shoulder and would remain fresh for many days, kept refrigerated at night.

We counted the money we had been given as gifts, $120 total, so that is what we had to work with for our short honeymoon. Not having planned ahead very well, we drove around quite a while, even into the area of the "Cities," and found no accommodations that we could afford or wished to stay in. We finally ended up in the area of Richardson, where I had danced many nights, staying in a small motel. We were up early, sun shining brightly (naturally) and decided to drive to Hayward, a popular summertime tourist destination and, coincidentally, "The Muskie Capital of the World." We stayed in a small, rustic cabin for only three nights, visiting the logging museum, the muskie museum, and also ate at Paul Bunyan's cafe and a cafe located in a train car. During this time in Hayward, I told Gene that if he ever laid a hand on me in the wrong way I would be gone. He came from a family of considerate people and his dad was a gentle, thoughtful man, so all of the sons became like him. I was determined to not have to live as my mother did. I had not told Gene about my background, and we didn't talk about that until many decades later. Today, I would perhaps handle that differently, more openly and honestly; but shame kept me from being truthful about all of my background.

We went back to Glenwood and spent a little more time with the Rivards, taking in a baseball game at the Twins ballpark. We ran out of gas on the way back while driving on I-94 east of Hudson, and while not pleasant at the time, we have often laughed about it since. We came back to DeKalb in time for me to begin my job on the last Monday in August and for Gene to open his store, Finn's Ltd., on September 1, 1965.

Gene would be in business in three different locations over the years until December 12, 1999, a total of thirty-four years, providing jobs and good, quality clothing for many others all that time. Customers drove in from the suburbs and Chicago and often flew in from around the country to receive the kind of service from Gene and his staff that was a rarity even then. By 1999, people no longer cared as much about their appearance as in the old days, and discount shopping centers attracted people in large numbers. It was hard for a small business such as Gene's to continue to be profitable; however, he certainly made his dream from 1963 come true. Hard work, long hours, and persistence paid off for him and his family. We all benefitted.

IN MY PROFESSIONAL SHOES

Throughout my professional career that spanned half a century (with the hiatus of sixteen years when I raised my four sons), I worked in eighteen different sites, in five school districts, with thousands of children ages three to eighteen, interacting with hundreds of teachers, other professional staff members, and parents.

My first "real" job was from late August 1965 until May 1969 in Central Community Unit School District # 301. I served 120 students in five schools in Burlington, Lily Lake, Plato Center, Udina, and the combined junior and senior high school. I loved this job more than any other and was there for four years. In the summer of 1966, I worked at NIU supervising undergraduate students in the DSCC (Division of Services for Crippled Children) summer camp program, then continued supervising some of them during their school practicum (called student teaching back then).

During my second year in District # 301, I carried my first-born son, Brian, the entire nine months, working all day on the very day he was born, two weeks early. I complained to everyone that day that my back was aching and tired as I went up and downstairs with children who were in my program in Burlington. I didn't know then that I was already in labor.

My work for the year was complete that day, and I said farewell to my students and teacher friends in both of my buildings. I had not used a single sick day in my two years and left Lily Lake around four, thinking that I would have two weeks of vacation to get ready as my baby was two weeks from its due date.

Just west of the intersection of Highways 47 and 64 is a long, gradual curve with a slight incline. Since May 4, 1967, members of our family have always referred to it as "Brian's Curve." As I was driving along, I felt a release of pressure and instantly realized that the whoosh I experienced was amniotic fluid. Luckily, our 1963 Bonneville that we drove at that time had a vinyl bench seat, and there was a box of Kleenex nearby that I used to absorb the portion that didn't drench my dress and undergarments. Stuffing the Kleenex up my dress and keeping my wits about myself, I thought silently, *I hope some nut doesn't run into me!*

I had eleven miles to drive to get to Sycamore and an additional six miles to DeKalb, and fortunately, nothing drastic happened. I remained calm even as I went into Gene's parents' house. "Vic, I have to go," I said. "Go where?" his mother asked. "To the hospital," I told her. She originally got frazzled, then made arrangements for her own child's care (she had had her last child at the age of forty-six, so he was still young), then drove me to our apartment to get the bag that I had already packed as I like being prepared ahead of time. I was totally unfamiliar with hospital procedures, having never been in one as a patient before, and didn't know if they would admit me on my own, so I asked Vic to accompany me. I was a novice in all of this.

I went immediately into hard labor as soon as I was admitted. "I see you got cheated out of that two-week vacation you thought you were going to have!" said my doctor. Gene arrived around six after closing his store but was not allowed into the delivery room, as was usual procedure in those days. Men were considered a hindrance by the medical personnel and kept away from the entire process. After a few hours of hard labor, Brian Michael was born at 8:53, "a red-headed little Irishman" with strawberry-blond hair, according to Dr. Feeney, and weighing five pounds, ten ounces—called a pipsqueak, according to Grandpa Finn.

I was able to stay home and care for Brian during that summer, then resumed my work in my same schools for two more years. Going to work in this district was a joy every day; however, I did miss caring for my son myself. The first year of Brian's life, Grandma Finn cared for him, and Anna, a former young adult student I had at NIU in my graduate program, cared for him the second. When we paid more in taxes than I earned, I asked to be released of my contract at the end of that school year. It was with great sadness that I left my first and favorite job; however, I was now in the best job any woman could ever have, that of motherhood.

Gene with Brian on his first birthday, May 4, 1968

Bev also with Brian, May 4, 1968

With the exception of helping out with preschool speech and language screenings, it would be sixteen years before I went back into my professional shoes again. I was not idle, however, for I was very active in the parent-teacher organization in my sons' school, developing and teaching volunteer lessons in art appreciation, lessons about Hawaii, the Caribbean, and the sea, in addition to showing my extensive seashell collection time after time in many classrooms. Teachers requested that I return year after year to present my lessons. I always presented them as if I were teaching for real, with attention-getting openers, audiovisual materials, and real objects as often as possible, and including the students in any discussions or question/answer sessions.

During this period of "not working," I was instrumental in conceiving, organizing, and producing three all-school productions, including the entire school, with parents, teachers, and children all being involved. Each of these productions was special in its own way; however, *Central, You're A Grand Old School* was my favorite, a takeoff on George M. Cohan's musicals. Our school district was redistricting and consolidating in order to save money, and Central School, the oldest of all the schools, was the one

...geted for closure. Instead of feeding into a sob story, we celebrated the wonders of what made Central so special. We hired a former Miss Illinois 1973, Colleen Metternich Puscas, to help us carry off this huge undertaking, and we paid her fee by selling our *Central School Keepsake Cookbook*. All parents, teachers, and kids were invited to submit their favorite recipes for inclusion. It was a big seller, and we reordered several times.

My friend Jan, also a former theater major, and I were, as the directors and the mistresses of ceremonies, dressed in top hat and tails, vests, red bow ties, fishnet stockings, and red bows on our dancing shoes. We talked a number of teachers and parents into being in our can-can line, wearing deep-jewel-colored satin skirts that we made from coat linings I got from one of Gene's manufacturers. We had comedy skits, lots of songs, and parodies written by Colleen. For over two hours, the fun and merrymaking went on, a true celebration of a school that would be no more. One of our parents organized one of the classes into performing "Movin' Right Along," the Kermit the Frog song, that expressed the attitude people adopted, instead of "Oh, Poor, Poor Pitiful Me."

Every year, my sons and I planted and maintained a huge garden and raspberry patch, sharing the wealth of produce with teachers and friends. When the Lord provided so abundantly, it was just right to share what we harvested. One season, one of our neighbors over fertilized and burned everything up in his garden, so we shared some of everything we had. That is what neighbors do, after all, especially when living in the country as we do. I used to tell my sons that the more we shared, the more we would be blessed with the next year.

Our years were full and busy and went by quickly. Before we knew it, our family of just one son grew to be four of them. Living next door to Gene's brother, Richard, and his family (naturally, of four girls) was like having eight kids plus the neighbor kids. Our homes had both been moved from DeKalb to rural Sycamore in the fall of 1967 and renovated. Gene's last location of his store was in the Junction Shopping Center that was developed on the land that the two homes had occupied. Some of the Sears Craftsman homes popular at that time in towns that had railroads running through them still stand on West Lincoln Highway in DeKalb.

Every two years or so or more often if needed, we would have a big dump-truck load of sand delivered to our yard for all the kids to play and fantasize in. Their Tonka trucks and other equipment were well used in all that sand and rusted by the time they no longer played with them. Entire complexes and large projects were built out there, sometimes with running water, and many hours in that kind of play helped our sons to become engineers, scientists, and biologists.

Sons & neighbor kids in sand pile. Gene's youngest brother, John, far left

My sons often raised sunflowers at the edge of the garden. One year, they grew to astounding heights. We cut down the largest one and took it in to the kindergarten class so that all the children could "climb the beanstalk" while we adults supported it. They talked about that for a long time. This was another example of a hands-on experience that we encouraged.

Sean with tall sunflower used as a "beanstalk" in kindergarten that year

We had a small pool that other kids would ask to swim in. I told them that with all those rows in the garden to weed, there was no one to supervise them, so we made a deal: if each of them took a row, when we finished I would watch them. Worked out great. They learned how to be productive and nurture living things, the garden got weeded, and then there was time for play. We had "summer school," which consisted of self-directed (though guided) learning, and the other kids would call or ask, "Are you having school today?" My sons had a very extensive list of things they wanted to learn about, which we kept posted and kept adding on to, and there were no restrictions. They ended up with a great deal of knowledge and vocabularies that were impressive for kids.

One of my sons' teachers told me that if children in the class didn't know the answer to a question, "those Finn boys always know." A good example of the consequences of their advanced understanding and knowledge was shared with me by my second son. His class members wondered about the large white clouds to the west that were nearly always present. They didn't know that they were caused by the nuclear energy plant about forty miles away. My son explained nuclear power to his classmates, including specific, detailed information about the atomic bomb. His teacher's wide eyes told him that it was highly irregular for a ten-year-old to have such advanced knowledge that even she didn't have and to be able to coherently and correctly share that information.

I considered going back to work ten years after I had last worked because there was such a shortage of speech and language pathologists in our area; however, we decided that it would be better for our family for me to remain in my wife and motherhood role. I spent all my time with my family, sewing for them, making special birthday cakes they requested, taking them to concerts and other events, and encouraging constant learning and knowledge. Back then, mothers did nearly all the work with children and the household (including all of the diaper changes, medical and dental appointments, and bathing), and there were no retreats or weekend getaways as there are now for young mothers. We were always available for our family members and in the home. I don't remember any of us ever complaining about how things were, we considered ourselves fortunate to be home with the children while our husbands were out in the work force.

In the early summer of 1985, that changed for us due to a diagnosis of a serious blood disorder of one of my sons. With a hemoglobin level that was critically low, we had to rush him in to Children's Memorial Hospital in Chicago for transfusions. Later, hearing the doctors at Duke University Medical Center tell us about paroxysmal nocturnal hemoglobinuria (PNH) was a sobering occurrence. I registered for nine graduate hours covering Language Development, Language Evaluations and Diagnostics, and Aphasia and Traumatic Brain Injury to update my knowledge and skills in case medical bills made it necessary for me to go back to work to help out financially.

After about six weeks into the fall semester, too late to drop the classes, I was offered two jobs within a week of each other. One job was in my former district, # 301, full-time, and the other was in Sycamore, my hometown, that was half-time at the junior and senior high schools.

It was hard to make a decision because I really liked my former district; however, I decided to go to work in Sycamore because the drive would be much shorter and I could remain in the classes at NIU. It was a very busy time, and I'm glad that my sons were the ages they were by then.

I continued to work in Sycamore, beginning full-time in 1988, serving at one time or another every school in the district until 2001, when I retired from my last school. That did not last long, however, for I was asked to return part-time and continued serving the students until spring of 2007. All during this time in Sycamore, I was known for my very professional, timely work and comprehensive, well-written reports. I conducted whole-group speech and language lessons in all the kindergarten rooms in my buildings and problem-solving, pragmatic-language lessons that dealt with the higher levels of language and critical thinking in other rooms in addition to a very full therapy caseload. One of my dear friends, a custodian in one of my buildings, once told me that I always had kids with me and was working, unlike some people.

The children looked forward with delight to my lessons, and parents told me on several occasions, even if their children were not on my caseload but in one of the rooms in which I presented whole group lessons, that the children enjoyed them. One boy told his mother, "Mom, Mrs. Finn always wears pretty dresses, and her shoes always match her dresses!" Megan, a little second-grade girl, always came to my office across the hall to see which heels I had worn that day and asked to try them on, telling me that when she was big, she would wear those kinds of shoes. I always wanted to be a good, positive model in every way for the children who saw me in their building. It was the least I could do to repay those teachers of my own from so long ago who had done the same thing for me. On more than one occasion, I was asked by people in my buildings if I happened to be the principal because I was always professionally and appropriately dressed. I also wanted to be appropriate in every way because some of my students, especially those with autism, were very sensitive to stimuli, especially scents. I did not wear heavy perfume, and always made sure that I did not offend them with odd fragrances. One day, after lunch, one of my students, very perceptive and sensitive, said to me: "You had tuna for lunch, didn't you?" As careful as I was, he caught that. Work with my students was never dull or boring but fun, rewarding and joyful.

A highlight of my efforts was in implementing Ellen Pritchard Dodge's program called The Communication Lab. This ten-week program teaches children the fundamentals of being a good communicator and covers areas not taught elsewhere in the curriculum. This program was requested by many of the teachers, and they would set up the schedule with me early in the year so it could be included. The children loved being involved in the role plays suggested in the plan, and parents were invited in for the last session to observe their children's improved communication skills.

When I learned that I would not be returning in my part-time position, I received a job offer that same day in another district from the administrator who had originally hired me in Sycamore and whom I admired and respected. Another retired speech and language pathologist and I would share the large caseload of Locust School in Marengo for a full school year.

The next year, I worked in the neighboring district that was totally comprised of just one school, kindergarten through eighth grade, in an older building with welcoming staff and superintendent/principal. One of my favorite memories is of this administrator, married to one of my colleagues in Sycamore, telling me during our discussion about the location of my room, "No, Little Miss Goldilocks, we can't *all* have the room we want." He did acquiesce, though, and I used the room in the front of the building with windows that allowed me to see parents as they drove in to pick up or drop off my students who came from home or were only there part of the day. Made perfect sense to me and was time-friendly for all. It had been a long, long time, though, since anyone called me "Little Miss Goldilocks."

I did not plan to work that following year as I was trying to organize slides for preservation on discs and document family history for my sons. In February, I got a phone call from the speech and language director in Rockford who knew a lady now in her district whom I had worked with the previous year. She had given Ann my name along with her recommendation. A young man, one of the rare male speech pathologists, just forty-two, did not survive surgery to install a port for dialysis, leaving a full caseload of forty students at the elementary level. I did not feel up to working every day, all day, in addition to driving the sixty-seven miles round-trip between my home and the school, so we compromised.

We worked the details out. I covered all the therapy sessions in three days of work, and other speech and language pathologists did the evaluations and attended the meetings that came up during the last three months of school. It worked out beautifully for everyone, especially the kids, who continued to receive the services they needed that were on their Individual Education Plans (IEPs).

The following year, I had planned to work in the spring, again in Rockford, in a school with over five hundred preschoolers, but when my son Brian was killed in a bad plane crash in California, I just couldn't do it. I felt crippled and unable to function properly, just going through the days like an automaton.

I did not work professionally again until the spring of 2012, working full-time for seven weeks, filling in for my friend who had foot surgery. Her caseload was comprised entirely of students who had been born deaf and who had cochlear implants. Just one student remained deaf, the decision of her family for her to remain in the culture of the deaf instead of floating between both the hearing population and the deaf as those with the implants are able to do.

I worked with this population again during the fall of 2012 when a young lady had her first baby. It was like coming home again, and it was nice for the students as we already knew each other from the springtime.

In a way, I have come full circle from my beginnings when my graduate work consisted of classes and therapy/teaching in both speech and hearing. There are always jobs out there for people in my field, which is satisfying. Doing good things for others was one of the goals of my early life, and I am proud to state that I have accomplished that with a flawless work record.

In the Kitchen...

Special sweetheart desserts for Valentine's Day

By Susan Eckman
Society Editor

Bev Finn

Bev Finn resides southwest of Sycamore with her husband, Eugene and their four sons, Brian, Darren, Brendon and Sean. Bev is the speech and language clinician at the Sycamore Junior High and the high school and still finds time to create delicious baked goods.

She has chosen some of her family's favorite desserts and a special Sweetheart coffee cake in honor of Valentine's Day. She hopes you will enjoy preparing and eating these delights.

By the way, Bev baked all of the delicious dishes so you also could view them. The Chocolate Mousse and the Sweetheart coffee cake were simply delicious.

Sweetheart Coffee Cake

2 pkgs. dry yeast (or two cakes)
¼ c. warm water with ½ c. sugar added
½ c. hot scalded milk
1 c. sugar
2 tsp. cinnamon
melted butter
½ c. sugar
3 unbeaten eggs
1 c. chopped walnuts
2 tsp. salt
½ c. butter or margarine
4½ to 5 c. sifted flour

Soften yeast in water to which ½ c. sugar has been added. In a large bowl, combine butter, ½ c. sugar, salt and milk. Stir to melt butter. Cool to lukewarm. Stir in eggs and yeast. Gradually add flour to form a stiff dough. Knead on floured surface until smooth and satiny, about 5 minutes.

Place in a greased bowl; cover. Let rise in a warm place until dough doubles in size about 1½ hours. Roll out half of the dough in 18 x 14 inch rectangle.

Brush with melted butter. Combine nuts, 1 c. sugar and cinnamon, sprinkle half over dough. Roll as for jelly roll, beginning with the 18 inch side. Place on a greased baking sheet. Fold half of roll on top of the other half; seal ends.

Starting at folded end, cut down center of roll to within 1-inch of the other end. Turn cut halves on side, cut side up to form a heart. Repeat with remaining dough.

Cover and let stand in warm place until dough doubles in size again. About 45 minutes. Preheat oven to 350 degrees and bake for 25 to 30 minutes. Makes two cakes.

Russian Tea Cakes

1 c. butter (or ½ c. butter & ½ c. oleo)
2 tsp. vanilla
½ c. powdered sugar
2 Tbs. water
3 c. sifted flour
1 c. finely chopped nuts

Cream butter, add sugar and cream together. Add vanilla and water. Slowly add flour and mix thoroughly. Stir in nuts. Shape

into tiny balls about the size of a "shooter" marble, drop by spoonfuls onto ungreased sheets.

Bake in slow 300 degrees oven for 25 minutes, or until lightly browned. Roll in powdered sugar while hot, and again when cool. (The second powdering is optional but the cakes do look more attractive if powdered a second time.

I usually use a strainer to shake sugar over the tops of the cookies. Handle gently so they don't get tough. These melt in your mouth

Quick and Easy Chocolate Mousse

2 c. (12 oz.) semi sweet chocolate chips
pinch of salt
1½ c. whipping cream, heated to boiling point
Whipped cream for topping (optional)
1½ tsp. vanilla
6 egg yolks
2 egg whites
Fresh violets or candied violets for garnish (optional)
Chocolate Dragonflies as a garnish (next recipe)

Combine chocolate, vanilla and salt in blender, or food processor fitted with steel knife, and mix 30 seconds. Add boiling cream and continue mixing 30 seconds more, or until chocolate is completely melted.

Add yolks and mix for 5 seconds. Transfer to bowl and allow to cool. Beat egg white until stiff peaks form. Gently fold into chocolate mixture.

Place in serving bowl, wine glasses or small clear glass dessert dishes. Cover with plastic wrap and chill. Garnish with fresh or candied violets or chocolate dragonflies.

Chocolate Dragonflies

8 oz. semisweet chocolate
Additional chocolate (optional)
Fine strips of angelica and candied cherries (optional)

Using a pencil, outline dragonflies onto sheet of waxed paper, then turn paper over so diagram shows through back. DO NOT CUT OUT. Melt chocolate over water in a double boiler. Place in parchment or foil decorating cone. Carefully trace outlines of wings with chocolate (do not fill in center of wings) Totally fill bodies.

Squiggle chocolate from side to side of wings, looping back and forth through middle and being sure each loop touches both sides of outline.

Repeat until desired numbers are made. Leaving the dragonflies on the wax paper, transfer to a baking sheet and refrigerate until firm. When firm, store in a covered container in refrigerator or freezer.

If desired use angelica for antennae and bits of candied cherries for eyes. Serve as a garnish on top of Chocolate Mousse.

Lemon Meringue Pie

½ c. cornstarch
2 Tbs. flour
1 c. sugar
1½ c. warm water
½ to ¾ c. lemon juice (Usually 2 lemons, needed but pulp included)
3 Tbs. butter
3 Tbs. sugar
¼ tsp. grated lemon rind (optional)
¼ tsp. salt
3 eggs, separated
Baked 9" pie shell

Original Recipe Wins First Prize

by NANCY LYNCH

What do you do if you can't find just the recipe you want? If you're like Beverly Finn, First Prize Winner in the Holiday Recipe Contest, you experiment and create your own.

Beverly's original creation of Triple Good Pumpkin Soup was this year's top winner. She developed the recipe a few years ago when she was to entertain guests and wanted something extra-special to serve. Says Bev, "I knew I had served my various home-made soups before, and I wanted something different, so I experimented with chunks of pumpkin and came up with the original version of pumpkin soup."

When cooking with fresh pumpkin, Beverly suggests that you make sure the pumpkin is the right variety for cooking. Burpee's Big Tom and Small Sugar varieties are suitable for cooking. Beverly bakes pumpkin in the oven like any type of squash, then scoops it out after cooking.

Beverly, who comes from a family of nine children, started cooking when she was about 10 years old. She enrolled in home economics classes during all four years of high school in Wisconsin, where she learned how to prepare well-balanced menus, and make meals that are attractive, colorful, and varying in texture and flavors.

Beverly and Gene Finn have four sons; Brian, 9; Darren, 6; Brendan, 5; and Sean, 3½. All of the boys help with the huge garden each year, as well as having their own special plots for planting. At season's end, Beverly cans and freezes, makes pickles and preserves. A speech therapist.

Beverly is secretary of the Kishwaukee Area Speech and Hearing Association and hopes to return to work after her four boys are older.

She loves to keep busy, and in addition to cooking and caring for her family, Beverly also does flower arrangements, makes wall plaques, felt wall-hangings, refinishes furniture, makes sea shell arrangements and sews.

Her sewing specialty is doing patchwork – quilts, pillow covers, chair covers, and clothing. Using squares of plaid wool, Beverly fashioned a colorful, lined patchwork cape.

Not one to be idle, Beverly is getting ready for next year's recipe contest. Says Bev, "I've already started working on a new dish using pumpkin puree, so I'm looking forward to entering next year's contest."

Among the recipes submitted by Beverly Finn was one for Pumpkin Go-Round Coffee Cake. Here Beverly drizzles icing over the coffee cake, fresh and warm from the oven. News Staff Photo

Bev in North School office, late 1990s

"GOOD FOR THE YOUNG, GOOD FOR THE OLD, GOOD FOR THE THREE-MONTH-OLD BABY TOO"

During the years that our sons were small and I was home with them full-time, we all looked forward to the special vacations we went on for several years in a row. We chose very beautiful vacation spots and did research and planning months ahead of the time we would take off. We approached this as if it were an assignment, studying and absorbing everything we could about our next destination. We lived a frugal lifestyle during the rest of the year in order to be able to afford this one great getaway. We did take our sons to special exhibits as they occurred, such as the King Tut display or to such esteemed museums as the Scripps Institution of Oceanography in California. On one trip, while Gene attended his convention of clothiers, I drove our sons to see the famous and impressive Hoover Dam.

Our first such vacation was in the early spring of 1971, when we had two sons and I was expecting a third baby the following fall. We planned a trip to New Orleans, along the gulf coast and into Texas through Corpus Christi, which had been devastated by a hurricane. We visited the Astrodome in Houston, drove through the King Ranch, which took forever to get through, down to Brownsville, stopped in San Antonio to see the Alamo and to walk along the canals, and on to Dallas. On the return trip, we passed through Little Rock to enjoy the hot springs before the long drive home. Our sons were no trouble for us, so we planned to take them again the next time we went on a special trip.

This next trip was in early 1972, a little over two months after our third son was born. We were interested in visiting Jamaica and read everything we could so that we could make an informed decision about where we would spend our time there. We flew into Montego Bay, loaded with extra suitcases full of diapers, baby food, and formula. We took our own disposable diapers when traveling because the quality of those not made in America was very poor and expensive, if available at all.

Darren asleep in Bev's arms, Doctors' Cave Beach, Jamaica, 1972

We stayed close to the famous and very lovely Doctor's Cave Beach, on the main strip of Montego Bay, up on the twentieth floor of a high-rise which had a balcony overlooking the beautiful Caribbean Sea. We often enjoyed breakfast, including melon and other abundant tropical fruits on the balcony. Nearly every day, like clockwork, around four o'clock in the afternoon, a thunderstorm moved in across the water, dropped its moisture, then dissipated. We were originally surprised by the frequency of these rainstorms but got used to them. We also got used to the frequent brownouts, which we were unprepared for, though we soon learned that that was a common way for the island to stretch out and conserve its electrical power. They also conserved the fresh rainwater that flowed off metal roofs and into barrels.

We snorkeled in the pure, clear water and taught Brian, at the age of four, how to enjoy this sport also. On one of his adventures snorkeling with Gene, they saw and held in their hands a tiny seahorse, one of nature's most intriguing and fascinating creatures and the highlight of swimming there. All around, of course, were the many varieties of vivid tropical fish and the numerous kinds of coral. Sometimes, we enjoyed viewing the coral reefs from a glass-bottomed boat, a thrill for our sons and us as well. For Midwesterners like us, this was a whole new world.

We drove over to Dunn's River Falls, near Ocho Rios, in a rented vehicle. With the condition of the roads being even worse than those in Illinois, sure enough, we had a flat tire. Not to worry. Immediately, we were surrounded by helpful, friendly Jamaicans, including some children, who insisted that we allow them to change the tire. The men would not accept any money from Gene, but did allow the children to have it.

After we viewed and climbed the falls we ate at the restaurant at Sign Great House, a facility that used to be a plantation. There was wonderful music and several young ladies who loved holding and playing with our second son, who was about a year and a half old, and charming even then. We took the donkey ride down the hill, one of the employees shielding our baby so that the sun would not burn him or hurt his eyes. This was fun, and the photos we have with the beautiful Blue Mountains in the background are a pleasant reminder of the time spent with these warm, gracious people.

On the way back to our accommodations, we stopped along the road to enjoy fresh coconut, willingly cut by one of the natives. The large machete that the man used was enough to make our sons' eyes widen in admiration (and some trepidation I would imagine). The Jamaicans were always accommodating and friendly, and we left with fond memories of all of them we were lucky enough to have met.

The famous Rose Hall Great House was one of our destinations on the way back. This is an elegant old restored plantation mansion, with a hair-raising ghost story of the "White Witch," Annie Palmer. Big eyes again as our sons listened to the docent's presentation about the slaves kept, tortured, and murdered by Annie and her lover, and Annie's voodoo spirit wandering the grounds.

The Sundowner Cafe on Negril Beach, Jamaica, 1972

Negril Beach, now very developed, was totally unspoiled when we were there. There was just one small restaurant, called the Sundowner close to the beach itself. With the red-and-white checked tablecloths, it was like a small picnic area. We had the beach to ourselves with the exception of a woman obstetrician from Canada. On the way back from Negril, we came upon a man who had stopped his car right in the middle of the road and was reading the newspaper. Like a texter before his time,

I suppose, not paying attention to his driving. *No problem,* he probably thought, ignoring us.

Among our favorite memories is the story about the Banana Boat Club, a bar or restaurant in Montego Bay. We actually never visited it, but cannot forget about it. There was a car with a megaphone system rigged up on the top that routinely went up and down the main street during the daytime past the beach and the building we were in. Quite often, we would hear the man inside the car broadcasting his advertisement for the club. He would say, "Come to the Banana Boat Club. Good for the young, good for the old, good for the three-month-old baby too!" When people would see us on the beach with our three sons, they would see our baby, who turned three months during our stay there, and say, "So *you're* the ones with the three-month-old baby!" Then, they would marvel that parents would go to the expense and trouble of bringing their small children on such a special vacation. People often made other comments, also, about our sons in later years when we had all four of them. Brian was always big for his age, and he was three years older than our second son. Our last three sons, having been born in quick succession, were the same size and height for a while. Our second son was small for his age, our third was average, and our fourth son was tall for his age. They all looked the same with their cornsilk blonde hair, blue eyes and cute faces, and people often asked if we had a set of triplets among them. "No", we would respond. Then they would say: "Well, you must have at least a set of twins there." "No, they were all single births, and we're lucky to have them."

On the nights that we ate at a fine restaurant and did not include our sons, we hired a young lady who had been recommended by the manager of the building we stayed in. Avis Macintosh, who lived in Hopewell, an area south of Montego Bay that not even she felt comfortable going into too late at night, desperately tried to convince us to take her back with us to live with us and to help with our sons. She wanted very much to leave the poverty she lived in. It would have been complicated to have done so, and we could not honor her plea, though she was a fine young lady who was skilled with our sons.

Our first three sons with Avis, Montego Bay, Jamaica, 1972

We traveled by train into the Blue Mountains, again finding new friends during the trip. John and Missy enjoyed entertaining and talking with our sons. Always, people were amazed that we had our children along as that was very uncommon in those days. We saw lines of colorful fabrics strung along the way beside the tracks and young mothers coming up to the train windows with outstretched hands, begging for money. Hard to forget a vision like that. Reminded me of my own poverty-stricken beginnings. Gene, generous as he is, always passed something on to them during the stops.

We decided in August of 1972 to spend our next vacation in the Florida Keys and all the way down to Key West, home of Hemingway, tropical, and warm, we thought. We planned all the details for time in the sun, but during the time we were there, in February 1973, it was downright cold. I was expecting our fourth child in mid-May of that year, still far enough off so that I could safely travel. After spending part of our time there in the Keys and at Disneyworld, chilled to the bone, Gene went into a travel agency and requested information about going somewhere else, maybe the Virgin Islands. The people there thought that he was a travel agent himself.

We were booked and on a flight out that very afternoon to the island of St. Thomas. We were able to be accommodated at the Sapphire Beach Hotel, a lovely spot at the very east end of the island, looking out to St. John and the British Virgin Islands. We had taken some of our sons' Tonka toys, so they were happy as clams, digging, loading, and hauling that gorgeous white, soft sand. One day, we went over to Cinnamon Bay, pristine and unspoiled at that time, on the island of St. John. We took the Red Hook ferry to Trunk Bay, an underwater snorkeling trail that was a popular destination.

Gene and sons, Sapphire Beach, St. Thomas, U.S. Virgin Islands, 1973

We met many nice people on St. Thomas, including Ethel and Merton, an older couple from New York, and a friendly, bronzed, young couple from Greece, wearing very large, impressive gold chains with attached coins. They had a young son who played right alongside our boys, all of them digging, hauling, pouring, and constructing their sand castles and other architectural and engineering wonders. One time when Gene and Brian were snorkeling, they met a young man with a speargun strapped to his leg on the outside of his wet suit. He speared a fish then proudly displayed it for others to see. Merton was snorkeling too, and he got hung up on the coral reef but was able to free himself, showing us the ugly gashes left as marks of his encounter.

At the Tea Tree Restaurant, Georgetown, Grand Cayman, 1974.
L to R: Darren, Bev holding Sean, Gene, Brian, Brendan

We always chose destinations that would be safe for our family, and our next trip was planned for Grand Cayman, an English island with an advanced financial system and many banks. This was in the spring of 1974, and some people thought that such a place didn't even exist. It does, though, and we spent three weeks in Georgetown, at the Seaview Hotel, in a cottage across the street from the main building. Our food and accommodations at that time cost fifty dollars a day, which was a great value, especially considering that our sons continued to wear patched hand-me-downs and secondhand clothes while playing at home.

We were not far from the Seven Mile Beach, a long expanse of sugar-fine, pure-white sand with gradual, sloping water to play and splash in. Our youngest son spent much of his time napping on the beach under the sea grapes, shaded from the hot Caribbean sun. His older brothers also occasionally napped in these peaceful enclaves on the sand, and one time, we enjoyed a picnic in such an area.

We had two difficult experiences during this vacation. Our youngest son, who was about eight months at that time, was very ill for several days with a high fever and other such symptoms. Luckily, he did recover, though we did not learn what the cause of that illness was. The other bad experience was when our second son was struck by a car while trying to cross the street to follow me to the cottage instead of staying with his dad and his brothers. Thankfully, the car was not going very fast. Immediately after he was struck, an English medical doctor staying at the Seaview was there to attend to him. We took him to the hospital, and other than a concussion, he was all right, and we took him back to the cottage with us. I stayed awake all night, monitoring him and worrying about residual effects.

The turtle farm, called Mariculture, was a place that all tourists visited to see the endangered green sea turtle. They had many tanks of turtles at various stages of growth, and the owners planned to release a certain number of the young turtles back into the sea to help perpetuate the species. The owners were looking for investors in their business, and we could see the potential of such a business, especially considering that turtle meat is delicious and could be a fine source of protein for people. After many years, and no return on his investment, Gene checked with authorities on the island who informed him that all Caymanian investors were "made whole," while American investors were left holding the bag.

We made one other poor decision on that island. We looked at the Birdcages, structures right on Seven Mile Beach, intended as living/rental units. The cost per unit at that time was forty thousand dollars, a fortune we thought, and unaffordable. In addition, we did not have that kind of money. Those properties are now valued in the millions, even over into the Cayman Kai area.

We returned to Grand Cayman in the spring of 1976, that time staying in the Holiday Inn, the only hotel on the beach at that time except for the Victoria House which was closer to Georgetown. A major winter storm had passed through shortly before our arrival, which produced huge, rolling and crashing waves that our sons appreciated. Now, many hotels/motels line the entire length of Seven Mile Beach, which no longer is as unadulterated as the years we enjoyed its beauty. Cruise ships routinely make stops on this island, dropping thousands of tourists onto the sand, changing its appearance forever.

Trips to California were enjoyed in 1977 and 1979, and we visited both southern and northern parts of the state. We spent time in San Francisco, Big Sur, Pebble Beach, the redwoods area, San Diego, Palm Springs (including going up the mountain on the tram through seven climactic changes), the Los Angeles area near the La Brea tar pits, and the obligatory visits to Knott's Berry Farm and Disneyland (the original), and Coronado Island.

One of our favorite travel memories is of the elegant Sunday Brunch in the Crown Room at the Hotel del Coronado that we took our sons to. We knew that we could always count on them to behave appropriately, so we did not hesitate in including them in this gorgeous venue, with four crown-shaped chandeliers, a woman harpist playing ethereal music, and white linens for the very special meal, topped off with all kinds of chocolate desserts, including chocolate mousse. We taught our sons early on not to intrude on others' space or privacy, and this time once again, they verified our faith in them and their behavior. Such fine young men, just aged three, four, six, and nine.

On Coronado Island near San Diego, Hotel del Coronado in background
(where the gorgeous Crown Room Sunday brunch was enjoyed).
L to R: Brendan, Gene, Darren, Brian, Bev, Sean

Our 1978 trip to Hawaii was special, as all our sons were now older and able to remember at least portions of this vacation. We flew into Los Angeles before continuing on to Honolulu, located on the most populated island of Oahu (known as the Gathering Place). We didn't stay here, choosing instead to go on to the island of Kauai (known as the Garden Isle), aptly named for its rich, lush vegetation everywhere.

Whale watching on catamaran off Lahaina, on Maui, Hawaii, 1978.
L to R: Darren, Bev, Brendan, Brian, Gene, Sean

Here, we stayed at the new Princeville Resort on the north side of the island near Hanalei Bay, not far from the restaurant and bar called Tahiti Nui, one of Jackie's favorite haunts. (Yes, the same one.) While sitting at the bar, a gentleman on my right, whom I did not know, said to me, "That man sitting next to you looks just like Gene Finn." "He *is* Gene Finn," I said then introduced myself, learning that the man was one of Gene's customers from DeKalb. Small world!

Hiking the Na Pali Cliffs, Kauai, Hawaii, 1978
(where we encountered the beautiful young lady, sans clothing)

It was on this island that we came across the young lady who looked like an Amazon. We were at the northwest edge of the island, hiking the trail along the Na Pali cliffs, a narrow and dangerous strip. Our sons knew, though, to be careful and to not stray off the well-worn path because the outcome would be severe, considering the height and roughness of the cliffs. Coming down the trail toward us was a sight to behold. This beautiful well-endowed lady was wearing nothing but her backpack. One of our sons remarked after she had passed, "Her feet must be all cut up, she didn't have any shoes on!" Ahh, the wonders of youth, learning about life.

We did go to Poipu Beach, at the southeast part of the island, and drove around the south side as far as we were allowed to go. The southwest part of the island, called Black Beach at that time with the squeaking black sand, we were told, had at one time been a military base and was off-limits to us. I don't believe that is so now.

Lumahai Beach on the north side of the island was where *South Pacific* was filmed, and we looked for "Hawaiian diamonds," which sometimes are tossed up onto the sand. Such stones are a form of obsidian created by the intense volcanic heat. I had a pair of earrings with small green "diamonds," and I always wore them with the rest of my authentic Hawaiian garb, including a lei, when presenting lessons for children, with swaying Hawaiian music in the background.

We learned about the tradition of wearing flowers, especially the hibiscus blossom, in the hair. According to one of the Hawaiian young ladies, the meaning is as follows: if one wears the blossom at the left side, it means that she is taken. If she wears it on the right, it means that she is looking. If she wears one on each side it means that she is taken but still looking, and if worn at the back of the head, that means "Follow me, I'm desperate!" We have often told that story to others when talking about Hawaii. Always good for a laugh.

The second week in Hawaii, we flew on to Maui and briefly lost Brian in the transfer at the airport. He was delivered to the other plane in time, thankfully, to continue on with us. On Maui, The Valley Isle named for the valley between two mountains, we stayed in a condo next to the Intercontinental Hotel, and as one would expect, it was very elegant and stylish. The condo we were in was at that same level, beautifully appointed and well laid out. We were just south of the port city of Lahaina, on the west side of the island, where tourists congregated to watch for the whales.

We did not drive around the northeast side of the island to Hana, where the Seven Pools and Charles Lindberg's home are located because of the long and winding road there. We spent our time with our sons either on the beach or on a catamaran, hoping to see the humpback whales, which were there at that time giving birth to their young and having fun before going back to their summer playground in Alaska. We did not see any whales; however, we do have a great photo of all of us taken out there on the catamaran.

Our last week was spent on "The Big Island" of Hawaii. We walked on the Black Sand Beach (and yes, it does squeak), viewed and smelled the stench of the sulfur of the volcano area of Kilauea, observed and walked through lava tubes and Desolation Trail, enjoyed the numerous waterfalls, and the lush gardens with their abundant tropical blossoms, and drove around the Parker Ranch, cattle grazing peacefully, as if they were in Wisconsin, on our way over to the Kona Coast.

Black sand beach on the Big Island of Hawaii, Gene & Sean

On the squeaking black sand beach,
L to R: Bev, Sean, Darren or Brendan, Brian.
Other son is out of the photo.

Our return trip took us from Hawaii into Honolulu then on to San Diego, where Gene parted from us to attend one of his conventions. My sons and I flew into Denver for a stopover before going on to O'Hare in Chicago. When we arrived, it was about twelve thirty in the night. I had to leave Brian (at the age of ten, nearly eleven) in charge of his brothers and the luggage to go and find the car. This would be unheard of now to leave children alone, even for a short time, in the middle of the night, with the dangers present everywhere; however, back then, it was safe. One of Gene's part-time employees had driven our trusty old Volvo station wagon in for his own flight out to meet up with Gene and was to have left it gassed up. Luckily, I noticed that the gas tank was very low and had an opportunity to fill it up at the service oasis near O'Hare for the drive back home. That was a long day, and we were all glad to be back in our own beds.

One of our favorite trips was during spring break of 1983. We planned a driving trip to New Orleans, with stops along the way. Gene took the first leg of the trip from Sycamore to Cairo, Illinois. I drove from Cairo to Memphis, and Brian drove through the rest of the night until we arrived in Jackson, Mississippi, in the early hours of Easter Sunday morning. He had his learner's permit and was already a good driver, so we trusted him with the lives of our entire family. We had Gene's diesel Audi Sedan, with the extremely comfortable seats, and our younger sons slept most of the way. Brian would one day work on the elegant Audi's electrical and sound system and drive one on the autobahn when in Germany on his many working trips.

The church we found in Jackson was filled entirely with black people, all properly and beautifully dressed to celebrate this special day, singing in their inimitable way to glorify our Lord. It was a wonderful way to commemorate Easter, amid the music and flowers of spring.

We stopped at Vicksburg to see the battlefield area, old cannons, and other items of the Civil War before going on to Natchez to view the stately plantation mansions and then to New Orleans. Bourbon Street, of course, was an eye-opener for our sons, and we fully enjoyed the beignets and chicory coffee popular in the French Quarter.

Gene took our sons on later trips occasionally without me due to my full-time employment. They went white-water rafting, fishing for muskies, to the California beach, and even on a short cruise one time. Their behavior continued on the same admirable path and remains so today. We have often had people comment to us about how well-behaved, kind, and thoughtful they are, with such impeccable manners.

Sons & Bev with coconut

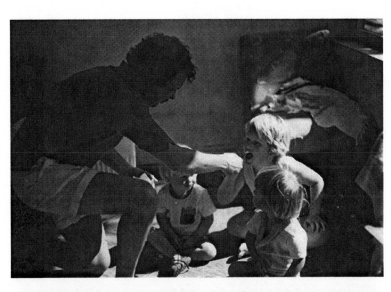

HEARTS AND ARMS OVERFLOWING

During my professional years, there were a number of times that I received thanks from parents and my students for my help. Many times there were heartfelt handwritten thank-you notes. Sometimes, delivered to the office, there would be a lovely bouquet along with a note from grateful parents for helping their child improve in speech and language skills along with developing self-assurance. Gifts were sent during the holidays, again with notes that I have kept in my special memory box.

The best gift of all happened when I least expected it. I had worked with a young boy for a year or more, three one-hour long sessions each week, helping him to overcome a severe case of childhood apraxia of speech. My student's home school was another of my sites, and I ordinarily would have fitted him into the schedule there; however, I was overloaded that year in that building. I suggested to his mother that if she could bring him to my other school, I could provide much more time on an individual basis. In addition, my room there in the new school was a regular big classroom so we could incorporate gross motor movement with our speech work. His mother, a dedicated and tireless advocate for her son, always stayed and observed the work I did with him so that she could help him at home. Both parents were determined that their son who, it was obvious, had a brilliant mind, would someday be able to express his thoughts. We did make progress, even though it is slow going any time there is a neurological or motor control component to the entire process of expressive speech.

One day, during a rare moment when I was not in a therapy session with students and was working on one of my professional reports, our school secretary contacted me through the intercom. In her dulcet voice and with the polished diction that all secretaries seem to possess, she said, "Mrs. Finn, can you come to the office, please?" "Certainly, I'll be right there," I replied. My room at that time was just across from the office, so I was there shortly. The sight that greeted me was a wonder to behold. There, in the office, stood both parents along with my young student, Michael, beaming, arms overflowing with many long-stemmed roses. "We got you peach 'cuz that's your favorite color," he said.

How is it possible to thank parents for such faith and gratitude? It was humbling to realize that Michael's parents went above and beyond to do the most that they could to help him achieve, and the roses were a symbol of their appreciation of the work I had done with their son. I don't know what happened to Michael, but if I had to guess, I would surmise that he is now working toward becoming an engineer. Michael had been held back by a severe disability but was able to gain some ground through early intervention and extremely dedicated parents. Another verification that I had chosen the right profession.

My students nearly always came to me after a long process of referral, meetings by the multidisciplinary team, parent contact, teacher involvement, and evaluation to determine eligibility. This was not the case with one of them. One year, in addition to two large elementary buildings to serve, another speech pathologist and I shared the middle-school caseload. My friend took sixth and seventh graders, and I served the eighth graders as that was an equitable distribution of the caseload in that building.

One day, one of the eighth graders not on the caseload came to see me in my office. I greeted him and was impressed that a student this age would venture to see me on his own. He introduced himself, and I asked him how I could help him. He said, "Mrs. Finn, I need your help." That surprised me as he was friendly and outgoing and a leader among his peers. "I need help because I stutter," he said with very few, if any, interruptions that I could observe at that time.

After contacting his parents, we conducted a speech and language case study and found him eligible according to guidelines we had to follow in the state of Illinois. Taped speech samples were analyzed, and a speech dysfluency count indicated a mild problem. Therapy sessions were set up and attended faithfully by the student, who made good progress. This young man is now a grown-up professional and family man himself. I saw him one time and chatted briefly with him. There was no remnant at all of that concerned young man of many years ago seeking help for himself.

My students made my days enjoyable, not only because of their unjaded view of the world, but often because of the precious things they would say. I will never forget one time when I asked a question of my kindergarten student who was working on improving his voice, and he quite innocently and honestly said: "Well, Mrs. Finn, I can't know everything!" After I smiled to myself and thought about the wisdom of that, I replied, "Nobody can, Daniel; we all do the best we can."

Another of my students, with a significant disability, would be so excited when her mother brought her to work with me that she always called out "FINN!" when she came in the building and saw me, then ran to me with open arms, anxious to get to work.

For some of my students, especially those who came out of troubled homes, I was their lifeline to hope of a better time. Even so, sometimes that wasn't enough. My greatest heartache and disappointment is that I could not prevent a student's suicide. One of my sixth grade students was small for his age and had a bad complexion in addition to his significant speech impediment. He was a target for jokes and teasing. He used to tell me that he planned to ride his bike in front of a big truck. I took his comments seriously and called a team meeting of all the professionals who served him. We learned that there were "no openings" in the schedule of the mental health facility in the larger town nearby that served my small community. This was at the end of the school year, so I was unable to follow up and keep pushing for help for my student. I learned during the summer that my student had hanged himself instead of riding in front of a truck. How sad, that professional mental health facilities cannot find time in a schedule to help a student desperately crying out for help and support.

Doing good, compassionate work was always important to me, and I am proud to say that I have a flawless work record. I am still called back to work occasionally to fill in for friends who have had surgery or babies. For two of my stints, I worked with students who had cochlear implants, an amazing surgery and technology that makes a world of difference for children who were born deaf. I was called on one time to take over a caseload of forty students of a young man who, unfortunately, did not survive surgery. His students talked about him often, always with great admiration. I was careful to reassure those students that the next fall they would have another speech teacher because I was going back to just being a grandma. I didn't want them to have to worry that another of their speech teachers had been taken from them. During the entire period, fifty years, that I have been in my field, we have never had enough of us for all the jobs out there, and I continually encourage young people to look into it if they have the skills and ability this profession requires.

"I WISH THAT WE HAD MORE HISTORY TOGETHER"

At the recent baptism of my niece's ten-week-old baby girl, the priest included a comment that I had to jot down. Luckily, I had a Post-it pad and pen in my coat pocket. He said that "history defines the present," and I was struck by how well that thought fit in with my last comments for my memoirs that I had written just a few days before.

As someone who has spent a lifetime in communication, I have always wanted to capture that elusive, fleeting aura that is present in a wonderfully complete conversation, to encapsulate the heart of a communicative exchange into a defining statement.

When it is time for me to leave this existence and go on to the next, I hope that I can remember the insightful, wistful words a dear friend and former colleague said to me when we last spent time together. It was a rushed, squeezed-in meeting, with our conversation far too short, and instead of talking about people or events, we talked about those weighty, significant topics some people are unwilling or unable to broach.

"I miss you. I miss seeing you. I wish that we had more history together."

"I do, too, my friend," my voice said, while my eyes said, "I understand."

I wish that we had more history together because we won't be coming back.

TAPESTRY OF A LIFETIME

It is hard to unravel the tapestry of a lifetime or to know all the threads that went into that lifetime. As I look back on mine, I am thankful that I had help all along the way and I was able to remain a survivor who moved out of poverty and into a life of a respected professional, as well as a wife and mother.

Profuse thanks must be given to my mother, who gave me life and my start in being skilled in language through her gifted recitation from memory of nursery rhymes and being a model for language without realizing it. Thanks too for her hard work so that I could have a better life.

Thanks to my biological siblings who lived through the same poverty I did and provided me with additional insight, clarified details, and jogged my memory on numerous occasions to help me tell our story as accurately as possible. And to my foster siblings, thanks for accepting me and including me as their "big sister, Bev."

Thanks to my husband, Gene, and my dear sons, the highlights of my life, for believing in me and encouraging me to tell my story—especially my second son, tenacious as he is. His words have been taken to heart by others, in addition to myself: "You have a sacred duty and a moral obligation to get this data written down. You need to write this for our family and for future generations."

I wholeheartedly thank and appreciate all my teachers. I was lucky to have gone to schools that had teachers who were competent, compassionate, and caring. All my teachers and professors cared about their students as individuals, regardless of their socioeconomic status or background.

Special thanks to all members of the large and enfolding Rivard family, especially Richard and Mary, who willingly took me in, accepted me, and treated me as one of their own. Without them, it is hard to know where I may have ended up.

Thanks to Miss Lillian Hartfiel, my fairy godmother, for keeping me on the right path.

I also thank all the good people of Wisconsin for providing the first three years of my college expenses until I reached the age of twenty-one. I was told that because my dad had paid into the Social Security system, I was able to receive help. I was on my own after then and had to work several part-time jobs and take out a loan to finish my last year at River Falls. I was fortunate enough to have received a teaching assistantship for my graduate work, though I still had to work part-time to cover all expenses.

That longtime debt is being repaid to my fellow Wisconsinites in a very special way. After my mother died, I established a perpetual endowed scholarship in her name at River Falls, in my field of communicative disorders. This scholarship is given each year to the outstanding Graduate Student of the Year as a financial gift to go along with the academic distinction. My mother would love that, as she had always wanted to continue her education but was not able to go beyond the eighth grade. She would love being "in college" forever.

Particular thanks to esteemed author/musician/humorist and fellow former Chippewa County resident Michael Perry, who—through telling his stories—heals us, inspires us, and helps the rest of us to tell ours. Thanks for sharing your special gifts, Michael.

Thanks to all my friends and colleagues who long ago convinced me that my story could help others in dire situations to have hope and to overcome. Big Bev, published author, was there at the beginning and provided early editing. Jerry and Ron, also authors themselves, set a good example. Terri helped me to realize that my story had merit and was worth sharing, especially with young ladies. Sue C., Sue L., Mary L., and Deb R. helped me to continue on my writing path. Paula and Harold, dear friends, encouraged me to set my goals higher.

To my longtime friends Julie, Judy, and Erma, heartfelt thanks for remaining my dear friends all these years. To Georgiann, though far away, thanks for constant support. Thanks to Michelle D. for early encouragement. Thanks to Cheri-Rose, with gifts of her own to share, for early input and suggestions.

Thanks to Toni (Dupey) Kenealy and her volunteers at the Cadott Area Historical Society for helping me locate, on numerous occasions, old newspaper articles and other information about my family and my hometown and for helping me to verify dates. In addition, thanks to the good people of Cadott of long ago who helped my family when we needed help.

Thanks to Don Bricker, Publisher of the Daily Chronicle in DeKalb for use of photos and text from out of the past.

Thanks to Sue P. and Sylvia B. for providing rooms of my own for my writing sabbaticals when I needed them for initial sorting, planning, and writing.

Thanks to Jim Mathis, photographer, for expert restoration and preservation of precious old photos and articles.

Thanks to Larry Easton, archivist for Soo Line Historical and Technical Society, for permission to include information about the Soo Line that ran through Cadott.

Thanks to Cadott School District Superintendent Joe Zydowsky and to Donna Thompson of Glenwood City High School for permission to use old photos and information found in yearbooks.

Thanks to everyone at Xlibris who helped me bring my dream to fruition, especially Mae, Michelle, Sarah, Clifford and Rita.

For a long time, I kept my background and childhood hidden and secret because I was ashamed of my dad and hated the miserable poverty I had to live in every day. I read fairy tales all the time to dream of and plan for a better life for myself. I never told people about my past because I thought it would adversely impact my efforts in pulling myself up by the bootstraps. People in college often asked me which foreign country I was from and asked questions such as "Are you some sort of countess?" I think the main reasons for their comments were that I was quiet, and therefore they perhaps thought mysterious, and I also had a defective /r/ sound, learned from my older sister, which made my speech pattern similar to that of a foreigner who did not speak English as her primary language. In addition, back then, I wore my long hair in elegant self-styled upsweeps, different every day. Thanks to people in my college experience who accepted me and included me.

Some of my classmates in Glenwood thought that I was an au pair for the Rivards. I was easily accepted by them and the adults of the town, in spite of my speech errors; but I think that the reason I was accepted was because I was living with the Rivards, leading members of the community, as Richard was an attorney and Mary, an artist and member of women's clubs. Thanks to all my classmates and the good people of Glenwood. You will always be in my heart.

The mother of a friend of my second son thought that I had come from a privileged background because of my skills and manner of presenting myself. She did not believe my son when he told her of my beginnings as she thought that I had been born with a silver spoon in my mouth. Far from it.

I believe that our Creator has a plan for each of us, just as Hans Christian Andersen said, "Every man's life is a fairy tale, written by the hands of God." It is amazing to me how many people come out of harsh environments and succeed in spite of hardships. People can get out of the culture of poverty and go on to live exemplary lives even though they began in desperate conditions.

It is my sincere wish that my story of fierce determination and the will to survive and achieve can provide hope and inspiration to young people, women especially, to fight against being a victim and to rise above their original conditions and situations and move on to a worthwhile life of serving others. Luck, of course, helps; and a good education, above all, can be their ticket out of poverty, just as it was for me. My good fortune in choosing my professional field has been a joy in my life. I am always proud to say that I am a speech-language pathologist and thankful that I did not have to live my life in poverty and degradation.

With many thanks to all who have helped me, and as dear Miss. Reece would say, "Cum amore." I'll gently leave it at that . . .

What you leave behind is not what is engraved in stone monuments, but what is woven into the lives of others.—Pericles

RESERVED FOR JEANNE

At the end of every school year back in the 1950s, young people exchanged their yearbooks for final thoughts and memories of the year just finished. Usually, these memories were brief comments about a specific class or event that happened during the year and were written by teachers as well as students.

My best friend from third grade until I left Cadott was Jeanne, whose father came to our small village as a coach and high school teacher. Jeanne wrote a full page in one and two and a half pages in another of my *Sagas*, the yearbook we both worked on in the business division of production. Her entries, included here, provide a glimpse of how high school girls communicated and thought in those days and reveal how important good friendships are. In addition, her comment about life being hedged in by commonplace but being able to live a large life in a little space is very insightful for a teenager.

Dear Bev,

Every time I try to think of something to write, my mind goes back to 3rd period in the 8th grade. We made some great stories for Mr. Collins, didn't we? Sleepy Hollow and others. Also, remember our great puppet theatre & our play "Plot To Kidnap Santa Claus" with me as Santa & Ann as Nancy, etc.; that night we went to Withee, our stage and running all over their high school. Were you scared??

And then, how about our plays, both of them. "Clue of The Red Ribbon" went off pretty good, didn't it, but "For Beauty's Sake" got stuck somewhere along the line, anyway, we stayed faithful until the end. The only trouble was that your parts always insult me. Sissy wasn't so mean though.

Remember the fun we had at the "All Girls Prom" Zowie!! Except you made fun at my "Bell Bottom Trousers". You made me mad!! (Not really!!!) Some of those crazy Horizon Girl parties. Especially that one at the old "Morg" (Sigel Town Hall) when the doorknob fell off and we locked Joan and Marianna inside and then we crawled back and forth out of the windows until Lyle Freagon came by and thought we were breaking in we ran then. Our Halloween parties were always fun, too. (Every kind was, Christmas, etc.).

You weren't in our Algebra class but I bet you had fun embarrassing Mr. Mott just like we did. Huh??

I bet we had the most fun in Civics with Mrs. Laurent. Hope we have her in W. History next year. In History we'll have fun again (I hope). As long as she doesn't give us as many tests as this year—year-year—(I use that word more often). Kind of poor English. Oh well Mrs. Gumz won't be reading this-. I can't remember much about how we met but we were just in third grade.

Remember the fun we had in grade school? I sure do! Mrs. Liddell was a lot of fun, Miss Freese (now Mrs. McConville) too. Mr. Collins took the cake, though. I'll never forget those days-not as long as I live.

The Prom!! Boy, don't forget that. Our wonderful punch & afterwards. I won't say anything about that cause I know you remember. Luck to a swell gal.

Jeanne

The following year, Jeanne wrote this:

Bev

Well 2 down—2 to go (years, I mean). After that, who knows? Anyway, no matter what happens, we've sure had fun haven't we??

We met first in 3rd grade—didn't get along so well at first either did we? But I remember a lot of things that have happened since then. Remember Owen and our puppet show? Man what a riot. In through the window—dum-de-dum (music notes). Or those fourth period study halls—anyway, we were supposed to study, you and I and Chuck and Morris. Remember Ann's little house? (and her church) she never did get that on straight.

Elvis—of course he's mine but we sure had fun arguing over him. All Shook Up!

Don't forget to come & visit me this summer. I doubt if I can introduce you to Dennis or those darlings because they will be gone. Boo Hoo! Not pleasant memories.

Celeste, Carol etc; they all bring funny things to mind. Even today, and poor Celeste ripping her ____s climbing over a fence. My feet ache now. Ouch! Ouch!

Remember the ballgames (basketball) especially when them flirtin' ones came in (and we were wearing our Elvis shirts). We'll be done in 2 days and I'll be gone but naturally I'll see you next year when we are good old Juniors at

C.H.S. Wish Renee was here to have fun with us.

Please excuse the sloppiness but I'm in a hurry! (So I can write a lot) Pencil, pen, etc, wish something would work.

Remember Rodney! We sure used to make him mad.

Turning to more serious thoughts, how about the Milwaukee County Hospital when we graduate? I'd better start saving now or I'll never make it.

Wish Miss Nelson was staying. We've had more fun and I still haven't met her brother Jackie. All Shook Up! (in squiggly writing). I can hear him now. Number 2!! I suppose someday we'll outgrow him but oh well—nothing has happened tomorrow—yet!!

Maybe next year you'll be going steady like Tommy Sands or maybe I will but we'll still have all the fun in the world.

You will have to go to the ballgames, football, too—with me. Every single one. Back to serious thoughts.

Your life is quite hedged in by commonplace yet you can live a large life in a little space. I don't think I'll ever forget it. Somehow it makes me think of Jeanne Loomer struggling through college or hoping to. Or you & I & Celeste together. Carol doesn't want to be a nurse but we love her anyway.

(then, in a circle, done like a campaign button is the following) I Like ELVIS

Boing!!! How'd you like to marry him!! I wouldn't not really—I'll take David or Denny any old day.

We've had a lot of fun with Mrs. Laurent these past 2 years—but never again! Unless one of us fails History—which I doubt. I'm getting writer's cramp but here goes.

There are a thousand things I could write about but right now I can't think of anything. Guess I'll close now! You probably remember the same things about our 8 years together that I do.

So—Farewell, Doll. I'll see you I guess this summer (don't forget) and we'll Rip It Up! So long—Farewell—Goodbye—Adios! See you soon.

Love from you know who "Elvis!" Me and you Heap Big Friends!!

Don't study too hard tonite: May 20th.

Hound Dog! Love Me! Don't Be Cruel! All sung by my guy, Elvis!! Tommy, Sal, Tab, etc. are all mine, toooo!!

Mr. W. was a pretty good English teacher, no?

RECOLLECTIONS AND ANSWERS

When my eldest son was in elementary school, one of his assignments was to interview an older member of his family. He chose to interview his Grandpa Finn and recorded the session. My sons (one, especially) have often questioned me about my life before they became part of it. This appendix is intended to add information that may have been omitted from the main portion of the book.

Because we lived our childhood lives when I was a kid according to the time of the year, we are using the format of the seasons merely as an organizational aide.

SPRING

Where did you live as a kid? What did you think about living there?

Most of my young life was spent at the southwest edge of Cadott, so it was like living in the country. I loved living there, as we had more exposure to nature than kids who lived in town. We were free to explore on our own, to go fishing or picking berries, to walk the tracks, to watch things grow, to pick wildflowers, hang out the laundry, observe the cows, and learn about the facts of life. There were some drawbacks, such as the long walk to school in the winter, and not having running water or indoor plumbing. We lived at the end of Poplar Street, which now extends farther south than before. New homes have sprung up and there are no remnants of the way of life I knew as a kid, except that Cadott is still a fairly small town.

Tell me about your childhood bedroom; did you have a view from a window?

I never had a bedroom or a bed of my own. We always lived in a meager space, first, in the old T-shaped house, where a basement was later dug on the site and where we lived for a while, then the "garage", a 12 X 24′ space that was used as a home. This small space was divided by a hanging curtain of sorts, roughly at the halfway point. There was a kitchen-living area to the east with the table and a few chairs, stove and (eventually) a small refrigerator and a sofa; the west end served as a bedroom with three beds. My mother slept with Irene and Marlene in a double bed because my dad was gone by then. My brothers, Ken, Jim, and Ed slept in a three-quarter sized bed, and Ruby and I slept on a narrow cot. We slept in spoon fashion, Ruby at my back, wrapped around me. Gladie and Louis were out of the house by this time. When I went to live in Glenwood City with Richard and Mary, I always shared rooms there, too; and always while a student at River Falls. When I lived at 1126 Pleasant St., and later, at 318 N. 1st. St. as a graduate student in DeKalb, I finally had a room and an apartment of my own.

What was your family living room like?

As a small kid, I remember living in the basement after the old T-shaped house. That old house had a front porch upon which Ruby and I pushed Ken in the baby buggy. The basement was always damp and cool and divided into a kitchen, a sleeping area and the root cellar which was filled each fall with wooden nail kegs of sand filled with carrots, parsnips, turnips, and rutabagas; onions, potatoes and squash were on the dirt floor.

The kitchen area was toward the southeast, root cellar to the northwest, fruit cellar to the northeast, and sleeping areas to the north, northwest, and south, under the cupola and stairs where our parents slept. There was nothing fancy as I recall, just basic, plain beds in which we were doubled or tripled up. The entire top of the basement was covered with heavy tar paper to keep water out. My mother cooked on an old wood burning stove with a reservoir for water and a shelf up above. Limited heat was provided by an old metal Ben Franklin-type stove.

How did your parents support you financially when you were a kid?

We lived in abject poverty all the time. Most of our clothes were hand-me-downs. I remember getting new shoes and two dresses each August before school. We also had to wear the brown long stockings that were kind of a tan color, rather than white, as most other girls wore, because they cost less. I think my dad made enough money when he worked, he just drank it up. He would go to the bars, get drunk, and others would take it from him or he would fritter it away. We had no nice place to live, no good furniture, no functioning car, and no out of season food. I don't remember going hungry; but Gladie does. We really did live off of the land and spent the summer like the ant in the fable about the ant and the grasshopper with the ant putting away food for the winter. There were no trips or vacations, of course. Going to Aunt Laura's with Aunt Millie was a treat. Aunt Laura lived in Eagle River, several hours northeast of us.

Tell me how your mother spent her days.

My mother worked extremely hard so that her family could survive. There was no time for "lunch" or "coffee" or volunteer activities. She was a true Lady Of The Land. Every day was full of hard, back-breaking work. I remember many days when her hands bled from all of the work. She had to wash laundry by hand in galvanized tubs and a washboard, and she had to hang the laundry outside. There was no dryer for her but the sun and the breezes. My mother canned, gardened, pumped and carried water, butchered the chickens, and numerous other jobs; but the hardest job of all, I think, was when she and my older siblings dug the basement with a pick ax, shovels, and a wheelbarrow. My mother told me that it took them four years to dig the basement. I don't know how she cared for all nine of us kids and did her work, too; however, there was still time for games and "language" instruction.

Where did your dad work and what did he do?

My dad was a stonemason, as his father was, and a carpenter. Some of his stonework remains on farms in the Cadott/Chippewa County area. He would work in chunks of time, often "going on a bender", blowing all of his wages or having it stolen by unscrupulous people. My dad also kept bees in hives on our land, trapped fur-bearing animals and tanned their hides, did some logging and odd jobs. We kids all learned how to use his tools, mixed cement, sand and water for concrete, laid stones and blocks, knew how to shingle a roof, and all the other jobs he did. We were fearless, and it's amazing that none of us was ever hurt too badly.

How did your mother look when she dressed up?

When I was a kid, my mother wore hand-me-downs and I don't recall that she bought herself a new outfit. Perhaps she did when I was small. My mother was always slender, so she never looked frumpy or old. We did like to ask her to show us her wedding dress and shoes. The dress, as I recall, had lots of small buttons and was tea length. The shoes were the style of Louis XIV with the very neat heel that came around again in the 1990's. After dad was gone, my mother was out and about more and always looked nice; but she still bought most of her things at thrift stores. Not a bad idea, as often brand-new items still with price tags can be found. I remember that our mother's cousin, Marie, who worked at Marshall Field's Department Store in Chicago, sent boxes of clothes once in a while, which we loved because they were very fine quality. My mother wore clunky, rather gaudy jewelry, always costume, and she never had any nice, valuable pieces. I wish that she could've enjoyed some really fine fabrics and jewels during her lifetime.

What kind of clothes did your dad wear?

My dad was always a mess and I don't ever recall seeing him really clean or dressed up. I do remember him shaving sometimes, using a mug with shaving soap and a nice bristle shaving brush. He used a straight-edged razor that he sharpened on his razor strop (and which he sometimes used to hit us with). He wore work clothes, overalls with bibs, denim or plaid shirts, long red union suits, especially during cold weather, and work shoes with wool or the old-fashioned "monkey stockings" with the red heels. He never bathed or changed his clothing too often, even though my mother did laundry nearly every day by hand in galvanized wash tubs and a washboard. It was his choice, I think, to go around like he did. He used to always want me to scratch his head, and I hated that job because it never smelled clean and in the winter he had dandruff. He wore many layers during the winter time to stay warm, and he did teach us about good layering.

What jobs did you have as a kid?

We always had to work, and when not working at home, we had to work for local farmers. We learned early that there is no free lunch, and that we had to work if we wanted to survive.

Did your family do anything special on weekends?

We never had any special days or weekends while I was in Cadott, except for the summertime picnics with our mother and family friend, Bill. During my time with the Rivards, though, we celebrated often. Big picnics, family get-togethers, and parties with people from Glenwood were always at the house, using the pool, drinking the beer in the "beer house", and enjoying barbeques on the lawn. The Rivard place was THE party place for many years.

What toys did you have?

We did not have any toys when we were kids. We did, however, have access to bats and balls and all of us played together on teams. We didn't have to be concerned about our "rights" or our esteem, because we all played together, all mixed in; and we learned about real life during our play. We took our lumps when we did poorly, and got accolades when we did well. We also played with jacks at school and we were very good at this, with amazing dexterity, speed, and skill. We used jump ropes, both single and double, and chanted all kinds of chants while jumping. I used a broom handle cut down or a stick to teach myself to twirl like a baton, which I always wanted to do. We used things around the house or garden to play with and often played mumblypeg. We were very good at aiming jack knives or regular sharp knives; and I credit that game for my ability to hit a wastebasket from far away. We also learned how to shoot a real 22 rifle by pinging off cans or bottles from fence posts. One other thing that we used to do quite a bit was to balance on the rails of the railroad tracks as we went from one place to another. We mainly worked, though, as kids.

What kind of houses did your grandparents live in?

I never knew my paternal grandparents and I don't know if I was ever in their home. We often visited my maternal grandparents, however. My mother took us there two or three times a week when the weather was nice. We always walked there, and sometimes Uncle Bill would drive us back home. Both sets of grandparents lived on farms, which was common back then. Grandpa and Grandma Martinek's farm was small and they had just a few cows. I think that they mainly farmed just enough to get by. The house my dad grew up in is still standing, along with the pump house and barn that his dad must have built (considering the very good masonry).

Did your parents encourage you to develop any special talents?

My mother taught me to nurture growing things and to be skilled in language activities. I also learned from her example to persevere, to work hard, and to be considerate of others. Those skills have served me well in my home life and professional shoes.

Do you have any gardening/decorating tips you can share?

The early crops that are "hardy", not "tender" can be planted quite early (as soon as the ground can be worked). It's great to have baby greens, onions, arugula, spinach, radishes and other cool crops early in the spring or summer. The frequent spring rains help to keep such plants tender and the cooler temperatures prevent them from getting bitter. I've always liked the saying: "When you have a garden, you have a future; and when you have a future, you have a life". I also have always picked fresh flowers to enjoy inside—even peonies in big vases, as in a five-star hotel, in full, riotous exuberance all over the house.

Do you like working outdoors? What jobs do you not like to do?

Picking berries, gardening, and cutting flowers would have to be my favorite outdoor work. When I was a kid, I never liked getting my hands dirty or sticky and avoided those kinds of jobs whenever I could. We used to do construction work, though, and I didn't mind working with tools or cement. We used to dig for worms and fish, and I didn't mind the dirt from those, except for the slime on the fish. The job of plucking wet feathers was yucky, and I didn't like that; but that fried chicken certainly tasted good!

What subjects did you like to study in school?

The language arts were always interesting to me, and I got good grades in them. I was able to learn history, science, social studies, and geography with no difficulty. I had to work at math, though, as it wasn't intuitive for me to like math concepts and problems. Performing in front of others was easy for me, and I liked being in plays, marching in the marching groups, and singing. The field of speech was a natural choice for me; and that ultimately became my life's work and joy.

Is there a sight or smell that makes you think of your childhood?

Rich, dark, warm, moist garden soil instantly reminds me of life and all of its mysteries. Mother Earth was our lifeline as kids; and we appreciated her rich abundance. I still enjoy this earthy odor as I garden each spring and summer. It is especially enjoyable after a warm spring rain. Nothing can quite match the wonder of growth before one's eyes. It was nice that we lived where there was enough land for two big gardens when I was a kid. Because of my experience, you guys could get knowledge firsthand about growth, nutrition, and the wondrous cycle of life. Our gardens when I was a kid were generally plowed and my mother had the hard job of making the land workable. When you guys were kids, we generally had our garden tilled and we had the big Gravely for a while, which Brian handled because he was big for his age, strong, and knowledgeable. During the spring of 2012, your dad commented to me when we were planting six fruit trees, "Don't you think, now that you're 70, you can give that up?" I told him: "No, all the more reason to plant!". And I continue to do so.

Tell me about when you cut our hair outside.

In warm weather, I cut your hair on the front porch and just let the hair blow away. Some time later, we found birds' nests (mainly of the cardinals) that had carefully been lined with beautiful blonde hair! One of our friends who's a teacher kept a nest for her collection that has Finn boys' hair included.

RECOLLECTIONS AND ANSWERS

SUMMER

Who named you?

My mother told me that she named me. Old-fashioned names were popular in 1941. My name means "dweller at the beaver meadow". Wisconsin also comes from a word, Wishkonsing, which means "place of the beaver". I never really cared for my name, but just got used to it. I have had several friends over the years with whom I share a name. I learned about Beverly Hills, California while a teenager; that helped somewhat to make my name seem more acceptable. While living at home until I was 16, my siblings called me "Queenie" because I always liked to read and they thought I was lazy and didn't want to work. I just didn't want to do the jobs that got my hands dirty, except for gardening. We all had nicknames, even though I am not fond of them.

What were your experiences with religion as a kid?

We never went to church as kids because my dad wouldn't let my mother go or to take us. After my dad disappeared, I remember going to the Methodist church with my friend, Jeanne Loomer. When I was in junior high, my mother went back to the Catholic Church which she went to as a younger person. It was my good luck that I was a Catholic at the age of 16. Because of that, I was sent to live with the Rivards. I loved the rituals and routines of a structured Christian life. In addition, we all revered Mother Nature as the supreme being. When I was about 12 or 13 we were all baptized and then confirmed from Irene on down. We got small prayer books called missiles that we used at mass. We liked the size of these missiles, which was similar to a deck of cards. The pages were lightweight and very thin, similar to parchment, and the edges were usually finished with gold leaf or gilt. The covers were usually black, although for a special occasion, such as a first communion or confirmation, a white one would be given as a gift. I loved these little books, as there were many prayers and articles about the saints which inspired me to be a better person.

Living the life of a Cristian kept me on the moral track and helped me to not get into trouble. Now, my religious views are broader and more inclusive; however, living a moral, thoughtful, generous life continues to be important to me. I am glad that there is a higher power to make sense of everything and to give hope that after we die there will be life after that. I remain hopeful and optimistic that life goes on and that we will all be reunited at some point. I had a good friend who had two heart attacks followed by open heart surgeries, and reported that there is a "tunnel of light" and much peace at the end of it. This friend died in the summer of 2011, and I wonder if he found that to be true. I think that souls are recycled and that all life is reincarnated. That perhaps accounts for those "old souls" in the world and the "young ones" who have yet to catch up.

Did you have a favorite pastime as a kid?

Reading was always enticing to me, as I knew that there was a better world than the one I lived in. Reading transported me to faraway places and fantasy existences and taught me about the kind of person I wanted to be and the type of life I wanted to live as an adult. We read by kerosene lamp in the winter time and read all summer long. Every Wednesday during the summer we went to school for different books, which was a great day for me! We had no books of our own, so it was wonderful that we could borrow them from the school library.

Having grown up in Wisconsin, did you ever milk a cow?

When we went to visit Grandma, we loved being around the cows and often tried to milk them. We were able to squirt some rich, warm milk into our mouths or at the cats, who always came around for a treat. I loved the warm earthy smell of the cows and their sweet breath. I don't remember ever milking a cow completely, but I think that the older kids did. We carried full pails into the house and watched and waited while the thick, rich cream rose to the top. That was used to make into butter and we always wanted to do that job even though it could take quite a while. Sometimes, Grandma put some cream into a glass jar that we shook so we could see the butter being formed, though she generally used the big wooden churn that she kept in a corner of her kitchen.

Did you kids have a playhouse or special play area?

The alfalfa field to the south of our house was an area we often went into to get away and to hide. With its feathery, airy leaves and lavender blossoms, it was a heavenly spot to drift and dream. Usually it was just Ruby, Ken and I who went there. Sometimes we would climb up on the pig shed to get away.

How did you learn to swim, and where did you swim as a kid?

We learned to swim by taking organized lessons at the park after dad disappeared. He never let us do anything when he was around. We all liked the lessons and spent many hot days in the Yellow River. The water was colored like Coke or root beer but I remember it as being very clean. The color probably came from the tamarack trees farther up the river from us. We also swam in Lake Wissota by Shaffer's land at the east end of the lake near Bateman. It's the same lake that is mentioned in Titanic by the character, Jack Dawson, though in 1912 it hadn't yet been made.

Did you visit relatives in the summer?

We visited Aunt Laura in Eagle River when Aunt Millie took us along. We loved visiting Aunt Laura because she was always positive. Another trip I went on was to Janesville with Aunt Millie and Uncle Julius (to babysit Millie's son, David) when they went to visit Uncle Bill and Aunt Sally. They never had any kids. That is too bad, as Uncle Bill had good musical talent, played several instruments, and was handsome. While there, I remember luxuriating in a big, regular bathtub, which I had never enjoyed before.

Did you play "dress up" as a kid?

We had many boxes of clothes Bill Shaffer brought us from his junk route or hand-me-downs from people in the area. My favorite was a yellow prom dress with a lace overlay that was very elegant, such as Alencon. We always had plenty of high heeled shoes to wear also, as we played; and we learned to walk very well in them while still young. Ruby and I were most interested in these play sessions which set in motion my astute fashion sense. I used to study pictures and ads in magazines to see how cultured, sophisticated, accomplished ladies looked, dressed, and carried themselves. My work in theater continued that critical observational skill.

What was your first job?

My very first job for money was babysitting the kids next door while their mother went to work at The Northern Colony that housed most of the disabled people in the northern Wisconsin area. This family lived to the north of us, so it was handy. The son and the daughter were pretty good kids, though one of my brothers told me that one time the boy hit him in the back of the head with a bat. Jim had seizures for a time and had to be on medication for that for a while.

While working for this lady, I saved all summer to be able to buy a pretty blue, gored skirt and a white blouse with a scooped, lacy neckline. It was a nice outfit for church or school. I also bought an elegant gray sheath with a white portrait collar and buttons down the front with my money. I'm wearing that dress in the old picture of my siblings and me when I was about 15 or 16. There was a store, called Three Sisters, that we would go to when checking to see what was available. We rode the Greyhound bus to Chippewa Falls and back. Generally, though, we went to a thrift shop or had clothing given to us.

What kind of athletic endeavors did you participate in as a kid?

After dad was gone, Bill Shaffer brought a blue bike from his junk route for all of us to share. We would ride up and down our gravel street and were proud when we learned how. I learned to water ski during the summer of 1959 when I worked at Basswood Lodge. Some very gracious people from Rockford, Illinois had a nice Chris-Craft boat and helped me learn. Long Lake was clean and big and I loved waterskiing. The Tommy Bartlett water-ski show in Wisconsin Dells was big then, and those skiers set a good example for me. I have not yet learned to snow ski, although many students at River Falls did; I also have not learned to sail. We did try rollerskating as kids and we used my classmate, Ann's, metal plates that were attached to the bottom of shoes by using a metal key to tighten them.

Did your family have a car?

We had no car when I was a kid until after my dad was gone, and then only for a short time. Gladie has told me that our dad did have some Junkers that sat in the yard but didn't run. Somehow, around 1954, my mother and Gladie got enough money for at least a down payment on a strange, little yellow or green car called a Willys. It was odd in size and shape, but could get at least some of us around. We didn't have the car long because someone sideswiped Gladie when she was coming back from Chippewa Falls.

Did your family ever do any camping?

As young kids, we never went anywhere except to Aunt Laura's. We did sleep on the grass on very hot nights, though. When I camped with the Rivards in the summer of 1960, we had a favorite meal, chuck roast fixed with dry onion soup mix in foil right in the charcoal. It was yummy, and the fresh mountain air enhanced our enjoyment. Grandpa Rivard always drove, grandma sat in the passenger seat, and all seven kids and I sat in back seats in the old Pontiac station wagon that was loaded down and had things tied down on top. I wasn't a big fan of camping as it's hard; but it is nice being out in nature.

How do you remember celebrating birthdays?

When I was a kid, we just commented on them verbally and once in a while had a plain cake (maybe my mother's delicious crumb cake). There were no parties like some kids have nowadays. Having a birthday in the summer also meant no celebrating at school. Irene had a cake made for her one year by Miss Freese and her mother, which I thought was really nice. In college I celebrated with my friends, especially when I turned

21 in 1962. When you guys were little, we always celebrated, though generally only with family members. I used to make you whatever kind of cake you wanted, and you never stumped me! I loved making those trucks, earth moving equipment, farm equipment, fire trucks, rockets, Mickey Mouse, and many others. I remember each of you on your day as clearly as the day you were born; and always try to call each of you every year at the precise minute you were born to wish you a happy day.

Do you have any special memories of the Fourth of July?

When you guys were little and we were in Glenwood over the 4th of July, we went several times to see the fireworks in Hudson over the St. Croix River. That was a lovely place up by the Indian mounds, which I had visited during my college days at River Falls. One year we had some good-sized fireworks set off in Rivards' back yard over the dam. That was a cold July 4th, though, so everyone wore jackets or coats. One summer, we went up to Milwaukee to see the fireworks after being at Summer fest. Those were the best I've ever seen and nothing has topped them yet. We planned ahead and got there early for good viewing. The ground shook with some shots and we could see the ground display very well, as we were sitting on a hill. Maybe you remember those spectacular fireworks, too.

Describe a perfect summer day.

Low humidity, not too hot, puffy white clouds in a blue sky. Nice gentle breeze. Free all day to enjoy the company of a favorite friend or lover in a meadow with picnic lunch with champagne and good music. No distractions or aggravations, including no bugs. No hurry, no worry. Lots of engaging poems to choose from. Rest in the afternoon and a relaxing dinner in an upscale restaurant followed by sunset viewing at a place like Troy Burne over the river or lake. A light dinner on the deck with a good wine would be nice if one were at home. As it would be summer, strawberry shortcake would top things off. Being out in nature is vital to the overall perfection. Maybe it would be nice to watch a favorite upbeat movie, have a nice relaxing bath, and read something positive and hopeful before drifting off to sleep. If I were still young, I would choose to be with my sons in the garden or picking berries, swimming, and enjoying their laughter. It depends on one's age what would be the perfect day. Oh! And viewing the aurora borealis would be nice, (with no mosquitoes).

RECOLLECTIONS AND ANSWERS

FALL

What were some fun things you did with friends in the fall?

In Wisconsin, most people went on hayrides and walks, and sometimes bobbed for apples during a fall party or dance. Bobbing for apples, by the way, is quite a difficult thing to do. When I was in college in River Falls, one of my favorite things to do was to walk in Glen Park, over the swinging bridge that spans the Kinnickinnic River, hiking along its banks to a wide meadow filled with wildflowers. This was a place to dream, and I often wish that I could remember the way there so I could go there again.

Were there any fads when you were young?

I don't remember any fads when I was in grade school; however, when I was in high school, the hula hoop was introduced. It was a big hit; and everyone tried to spin one or more around all parts of their body. Elvis was also considered just a fad at the beginning. I loved Elvis from the start and remain a fan today. I had a pair of black jeans, a tee shirt with Elvis' picture on it, a little black hat with a small brim, and a ring that I wore quite often, especially to home ball games. Some of my friends had these, too. I still have the old ring, just a cheap thing with a picture of Elvis under a domed plastic magnifying portion. Rock and Roll started during my teen years during the 50s and I was carried along like every other teenager on the rhythmic, pulsing, upbeat music.

I liked all the singers and groups, and met Conway Twitty when I was in college. I have some pictures I took of him when he was young, thin, and handsome. I regret that I never saw Elvis in person, or Waylon Jennings. I also regret that I eventually threw my big, comprehensive Elvis scrapbook away, thinking that I was too old for such drivel. I wonder where that could be now if I hadn't been encouraged to throw it out, maybe in some collection. Every time I do throw something away, I invariably need it soon after; I guess that's why I hate to part with things and could be considered a pack rat. It could be a vestige of my younger days, too, when we saved and used everything.

Did you have a favorite teacher?

I really liked all of my teachers, especially Miss Freese and Mr. Collins; however, if I had to pick just one, Mrs. Eunice Liddell would be my choice. She taught 3rd and 4th grades in Cadott. That was her life because she and her husband, Earl, could not have their own children. She told me that some time in the 80's when I would visit her often when I was up in Wisconsin to see my mother. She told me that she considered all of us students her kids. She was inspiring and patient and very professional. I loved her gray streak at the front of her dark, wavy hair. Her voice was low and resonant and her manner was kind and helpful. She inspired me to go into the field of teaching. From third grade on, I knew that I wanted to be some kind of teacher who worked with words. How lucky I was to have found my field in River Falls, dealing with not only words, but phonetics, semantics, and language, as well.

How far did you live from school?

We lived eight-tenths of a mile from school, so we walked 3.2 miles each day, as we went home for lunch. We were all slender and strong from all of this continual exercise. Sometimes we took different routes through town or dawdled along the way, especially in the early spring when the ice broke and we used to dam up the creek. We had grades one through twelve in the same big brick building at first then a new one-story addition was built. I ended up in the old part again after the fifth through eighth grades in the newer one. I was in high school in Cadott for my freshman and sophomore years and until October of my junior year when I went to Glenwood City. In Glenwood, I rode the bus to school or got a ride with farm kids occasionally who drove by. Sometimes I walked, as school wasn't real far from the Rivards at that time.

What was the hardest thing you ever had to do?

Leaving home at the age of 16, never to return was probably the most difficult thing I ever had to face until I had to deal with the tragic loss of Brian in 2010. Losing my son has been like existing in a nightmare, except that it never ends.

Who taught you to sew and cook?

Every girl learned to sew in the old days. We sewed because that way we could have nicer clothing at less cost. We learned to make children's clothing, to re-make an item into another, to sew draperies, diapers, costumes, or whatever was needed. Nearly all of us took Home Economics (called Home Ec) and some of us took it all four years of high school, even though we were in college prep courses. We learned decorating, home management, food preparation and preserving, child care, and everything else dealing with being a competent wife and mother, which is what we all aspired to. Young ladies mainly considered becoming teachers, nurses, or secretaries back then; we didn't have the world open to us (or at least we didn't consider that back then).

What fashions were popular when you were young?

We wore the famous poodle skirt made of real woolen felt which had an applique of a poodle on a leash. Some were very fancy. Mine was turquoise with a white poodle. We also wore black and white saddle shoes, sweater sets, real fur collars, Peter Pan collars, and bobby socks rolled down several times at the ankles. Sometimes we wore white low top tennis shoes or oxfords. Rarely did we girls wear slacks or jeans. We were always dressed appropriately in coordinated outfits. When we wore nylons (before pantyhose were invented) the seams had to be absolutely and perfectly straight up the backs of the legs. We wore skirts and blouses and dresses most of the time. Sweats had not yet become accepted as street wear and jeans were worn only occasionally.

Did you do things your parents wouldn't have liked when you were young?

I never really did anything I was not supposed to. I didn't even date in high school. In college we were exposed to drinking beer and smoking cigarettes. Drugs really were not used that I know of except for some wild guys in college who used Benzedrine or something similar. I had no information about why or how they used it; and I did not go around with those guys. It was a big deal to have an ID card so that we could get into the beer joints for beer. We were not interested in going to the 21 or older bars. We went to Shady Grove near Beldenville and Shady Rest near Wilson, southeast of Glenwood, and also to dance halls that were separated according to age. In college, I spent time with other theatre people, who often were considered suspect in their behavior or looks by people who weren't associated with them.

What was your first date like?

I don't remember a first date, as we always went in groups to movies, to dances, to the beach, or out to eat. I never dated until I was 18 and in college because I was shy and socially immature because of my background. I never had trouble getting a date, though; and had more than my share of handsome, bright, nice young men who wanted to be with me. As I grew and matured, I became quite polished and intriguing to others. People thought that I was a foreigner, perhaps because of my polished diction and my theatrical training. I loved the knowledge of being alluring to others and someone who could be an interesting conversational partner and date. My education was a definite asset. I learned to show a true interest in the other person and not to spend so much time talking about my own interests.

Is there something you wish you had done when you were young?

I wish that I had had roller skates to learn that skill better. We never could afford any. When I got older, at the Rivards, I taught myself to ice skate though, and continued that sport even into adulthood. I taught Brian to ice skate at the NIU lagoon. I don't know why you other guys didn't try. Maybe because I got older. One of my sons learned to skate and play hockey with his friends. I wish that I had learned social skills a little earlier than I did because I was slow in that area.

Who would you say influenced you a great deal?

Dr. Blanche Davis was my speech and theater professor at River Falls. Everyone respected her immensely. She was very productive in helping each of us in speech to be the very best we could be. She advised us to get our proteins for our strength and to take care of ourselves. She taught us to be observant and had high expectations for us. She did not marry, until she was 65 and retired, and that was to a former sweetheart who was a National Geographics photographer. They had over 25 years together. The theater on the River Falls campus is named in her honor. What a great lady!

Who was your best childhood friend?

My class was small, just five of us girls and three boys, so we all played together. From grade three, my best friend was Jeanne. We wrote puppet shows and plays together in Mr. Collins' room. I often wonder what happened to those, as we spent a lot of time writing them. Kids back then were always productive and didn't complain about being bored. I lost track of Jeanne after she was in college in Eau Claire, but I learned at one of our reunions in Cadott that she died in San Francisco.

Why did you choose the colleges you went to?

River Falls was the only college I ever considered at the undergraduate level, and never regretted that decision. When I knew that I wanted to do graduate work in my field, I applied to several universities, including Stanford in Palo Alto and I had been accepted there. I chose NIU because they gave me a teaching assistantship of $220 a month. In exchange for that, I taught severely speech and/or hearing handicapped young adults 20 hours a week, took over for instructors on occasion, proctored tests, and conducted hearing and hearing aid evaluations, while carrying my several classes each semester. NIU was only 8 hours from family in Wisconsin at that time because the freeway had not been finished yet; so that's why I chose it. I also didn't want to be too far away from my family if there should be an emergency. So, I met dad as a result of coming to NIU. When I told Brian one time that I had been accepted at Stanford, he was astounded that I did not choose to go there. Ironically, he lived his last years in the Palo Alto area.

Did you ever go on a spectacular trip when you were younger?

When I was at NIU, I would travel back to St. Paul by train. The Burlington-Northern (or Great Northern, I can't remember for sure). Either Andre or Rollie would come to get me. Traveling along the Mississippi was great, and the scenery was spectacular. I love that very elegant way of traveling. It was also affordable, as I recall. Dad would drive me to Rochelle where I caught the train for St. Paul. Sometimes, I came the reverse route. One time, I flew back from The Cities to Chicago, and the only seat that was available was in first class. That was very nice! I've never flown that class again, however.

How did dad propose to you?

I don't remember that dad officially proposed to me. We did talk, though, about the future; and when the possibility of us getting married came up in the conversation, I told him that I did not want to be married to a bartender and that he had a lot more potential than that. He proved to everyone, most of all to himself, that he could fulfill his dream.

Where did you live after you and dad were married?

We lived at 318 N. First St., Apt. 2 in the Finn Apartments that Grandpa built in 1964 after their big stone home burned in December of 1963. They are still standing, like a big "V", close together at the back, and apart nearer the street. They are brick, and very well constructed. We had to leave there when we had Brian because there were no babies or kids allowed in the adults only buildings. This was a good location, and dad often walked to work when I had the only car to drive to my schools. I had been the first occupant in the south building, west basement apartment. They opened early in 1965, and I lived there with my friend, Donna, whom I had lived with on Lucinda Avenue just across from the Speech and Hearing Clinic. This was a big step up from my old, over-used basement apartment on Pleasant Street. Dad moved in after we were married, as people did not live together then who were not married. Things were a lot different then. The apartment had only one bedroom in addition to kitchen/dining room, bathroom, and living room. The apartments had radiant heat in the ceilings, which was a radical concept then. Now there is radiant heat available in floors. We had a carport in the back for the car but no garage or storage.

Do you know about our house being moved?

When Grandpa Finn and dad were involved with other businessmen in developing The Junction Shopping Center, there were two houses on that land on West Lincoln Hwy. in DeKalb. It would have cost as much to tear them down as it did to move them, so Grandpa arranged for both houses to be moved out where they are now, a move of about 7 or 8 miles. The move was begun on Columbus Day in 1967 and completed the next day. I was off of school that first day, so could watch the procedure while holding Brian. The police and Commonwealth Edison were in charge of the move of the houses on big tires (called "dollies") pulled by powerful trucks. The houses were moved onto what had been a field of corn, that happened to be low land, close to Hwy. 64. Because it had been a wet fall, the houses couldn't be moved all the way to the south of the cul—de-sac gravel lane, as intended, so were placed near the road, side by side from north to south, on what would come to be known as Shannon Lane.

HEAVY TRAFFIC — Anyone traveling on Annie Glidden Road Wednesday saw an uncommon sight. Occasionally a house is seen on this road but a pair traveling together requires a second glance. The pair are headed for a new lot on Route 64. *Oct. '67*

Dad and I were interested in buying one of the houses because we had to move out of the apartment. We liked the new location as well as the openness and many windows of the frame, wooden house we chose, that all of you grew up in, and we still live in. Uncle Richard and Aunt Sue had a house in DeKalb that was quite small, so Grandpa convinced them to purchase the other one, a large brick house. We have a picture that was in the DeKalb Daily Chronicle back then (and I intend to put it in my book, too) Both of these houses are Sears Craftsman Homes, as many of the homes are in towns that had a railroad running through it (as DeKalb does).

At one time, in its former location, a minister and his wife lived in the house with their eleven children. One summer, several of those children, now adults, came out to visit and reminisce about their experiences in the house, and they were glad that we saved and renovated it. They told of "pennies from Heaven" (thrown from the bannister), the location of the only bathroom in the house (that is now my working closet), and about one of the downstairs bedrooms that was their dad's study where he wrote his sermons (and that is now our "Finn Spa", according to Fiona).

We had saved enough for the down payment on the total cost of $25,000; and we made payments of $215.80 a month. Over the years, the house has been remodeled or renovated three times and re-roofed; but the beauty of the time period of 1927 remains inside. Such beauty includes the nine foot ceilings, the two built in Deacon's benches, the original front doors with beveled glass panels, the original milk glass chandelier in the dining room, the French doors between the dining and living rooms, several small, clear, leaded glass windows, built-in book case with the same clear, leaded glass doors, huge storage areas and closets, and the original oak woodwork and hardwood floors throughout. As a point of interest, not a single thing was damaged in either of the houses during the move. Amazing.

RECOLLECTIONS AND ANSWERS

WINTER

Were winters in Wisconsin when you were a kid similar to what they are here?

They were very long and severe. Every winter was a challenge. We always dealt with frostbite, even though we wore long johns, extra mittens, scarves and muffs. The muffs were very warm, usually made of rabbit fur. Many days we walked to school in sub-zero weather—to say nothing about what the wind chill must have been. That feature was never considered back then. Even though it was so cold and daunting, school was never cancelled and we always played outside during recess. Tall snow banks were along the roads and streets all winter long, and there was rarely a "January thaw". The long winters were followed by the ice breaking up on the river with a very loud crunching and banging, and people said that the "ice went out" (if I recall correctly). The warmth, newness, and fragrance of springtime, which arrived next made the harsh winters bearable.

Did you have pets when you were a kid?

We had a cat named Boots when I was around 8 or 10. She was gray and white with white paws and white on her chest (looked much like the Boots we had in the 90's). I also had a pet bunny, and wrote a poem in third grade about him. We had a cat, Tiger, who came home one winter day with part of his front paw missing. He had gotten caught in a trap. Many people trapped animals for extra income back then. My dad did, too; and we helped with the scraping, tanning, and stretching of hides. Tiger's paw healed as a stub with no intervention. We had a dog, named Lady, a nice German shepherd, and also had a dog named Pal for a while. At one time, we had a chicken, a big, plump white one named Arabella, that we considered a pet because she allowed us to pick her up and pet her.

Did you celebrate Valentine's Day in school?

Years ago, we had to give valentines to everyone in the class or room. No one was left out. We loved making and decorating the big box that they all went into; then someone would deliver them and we would have treats. Valentines were quite small then, and always had their own envelope. There was always a bigger, special one for the teacher in the packages sold. After I was grown up and married, dad always brought roses or other fresh flowers. The Lions Club used to sell a dozen red roses to each customer as a way of raising money for their undertakings. Dad, as a businessman, was always targeted for sales.

Did you have a collection when you were growing up?

I don't remember having any when I was a kid; but as an adult, I worked on a collection of lovely sea shells. We gathered quite a good variety during our years of going to the Caribbean. You may remember that I used to go into various classrooms and show the kids the collection and teach them a great lesson. I used to cover a table with aqua felt to resemble ocean water and I placed the shells, coral, and other items from the sea on that. The teachers loved when I did that lesson for them, and they asked me back repeatedly. Those were the years I was "just a mother" and "not working". I also had back sand from Hawaii and soft white, powdery sand from the Caribbean that the kids liked to feel and let run through their fingers. The favorite shell of the kids used to be the bleeding tooth shell (a little periwinkle-type of shell belonging to the nerites); and they also were impressed with the puffer fish and sea urchins because of their sharp spines. In addition to the sea and seashell lessons, I was a "Picture Lady" and taught art appreciation lessons for many years in addition to lessons about Hawaii and the Caribbean islands.

What good advice did you get from someone when you were young?

The best advice I ever got was from my mother: "Get a good education; it's something no one can ever take away from you." I could see the value of that in my quest to get out of poverty. In addition to my mother, I also got good advice from my teachers and Miss. Hartfiel, and excellent guidance from Richard and Mary. My teachers believed in me and let me know that my ability could help me to achieve significant levels of education. One time, though, Mr. Hoffman, my typing teacher in Cadott, wrote in my yearbook: "I wish you could have been a better typist." I wish I could have, also.

Did churches and schools have potlucks back then?

I don't remember these when I was small; however, when you guys were in school at Central, we often went. Those Central School mothers and staff were excellent cooks; and we organized a Keepsake Cookbook when Central was closed for students. The potlucks were always lots of fun and there was plenty to eat of everyone's favorite dishes. Even some of the fathers and kids brought their specialties. I was always helping and involved in the potlucks and could rely on you boys to behave appropriately when I was busy serving or in the kitchen with all of the other parent volunteers.

Tell about some good speakers you have heard.

While at River Falls, John F. Kennedy came to the area three times during the primary season. He was a brilliant communicator who gave people hope. Many of my friends at River Falls are exceptional speakers in their own right. Randy Pausch, of Carnegie-Mellon, who died in '08 at a young age, presented his "Last Lecture" which I saw on tape. As his real last lecture, it was exciting and sad at the same time because he left a wife and three beautiful children along with his recommendations for truly living one's life to the fullest.

Who in our family served in the military?

Grandpa Richard was in the Army during World War II. He was on Kodiak Island and in the Battle of the Bulge. Just recently, all of his journals during all of the war years, were donated to the library at the University in

River Falls. He was a wonderful writer, and I am looking forward to going there some time when I am back there to see them. My brother, Louis, was in the Army after he dropped out of high school. He was at Fort Leonard Wood, Missouri. While he was in the service, he got a big tattoo on his upper arm of a pretty lady wearing cowboy boots and nothing else. When he would move his arm a certain way, it looked as if the young lady would dance or wiggle. My sister's son, Jeff, was in the service and National Guard and has served two tours of duty to Iraq, as he is a first responder/EMT. My sister, Ruby, was in the Air Force. She joined right after high school and got her dental training there. Granda Finn was never in the service because he had three children and worked at the Green River defense plant in Dixon. Dad and his brothers, Don and Richard, were all in the Navy. Dad served as a dispersing clerk, was on a submarine in the Caribbean and Cuba, and on the Valley Forge aircraft carrier. And, of course, we know about our own family member serving in the Marine Corps and being in Desert Shield/ Storm. That was a hard time for me and I got a lot of gray hairs from worrying about his safety. What a relief when he got out of the service, and it was even better when he drove that van back home.

What was the nicest event you ever attended?

We were lucky enough to have been invited to a black tie wedding in Philadelphia when the son of one of dad's friends was marrying a young lady whose parents owned a major trucking line out there. I bought an elegant long black beaded gown and felt like a movie star while wearing it; dad wore his tuxedo, and looked, once again, like the model he had been in his younger years. Everything was five star at the gorgeous Four Seasons Hotel there. We were greeted with arrival bags of goodies and other assorted niceties, a full evening of dining and good times (with all the people in the wedding party speaking and sharing anecdotes). The full scale celebration the next evening took place among flowers everywhere that had been flown in from New York. Dining went on for hours, at stations for hors d oeuvres, then a full sit down dinner with wine and champagne and elegant desserts and wedding cake. The dance that followed was like being entertained by The Supremes and all of the singing groups from the 1960's. The following morning, there was a full brunch for those of us from out of town before leaving for the airport. This was an event to remember, and the most elegant wedding I have ever attended. We were fortunate to have been invited.

Gene & Bev at elegant wedding in Philadelphia, 1995.

What is one thing you are most glad that you tried?

One thing I'm very glad I did was to be involved in the theater and play productions in high school and college. Those productions gave me confidence and poise and helped me to realize how strong I can be in front of groups or speaking. I am glad that Dr. Davis helped us to present ourselves well and to become observant learners. I'm also glad that I tried synchronized swimming, SCUBA diving, twirling a baton, and learning to cook and sew at a young age.

One thing that I'm glad I tried was just a few years ago, when Brian encouraged me to ride his tandem bike with him. I was afraid of falling and causing him to fall, too, but got the hang of it. Brian told me that I was a good "stoker" because I have strong legs. As the "captain", he had to be responsible for both of us remaining upright. After several shorter rides for practice, we biked on Canada Road, south of Redwood City. The road was closed to traffic one Sunday morning so that bikers could ride along the Upper Crystal Springs Reservoir. With a gorgeous view from above looking all the way down the road, this was a ride like being on a magic carpet. At the end of this ride was the stately and peaceful Pulgas Water Temple, which we visited before going on the return ride.

What are you thankful for?

I am thankful for the good beginning my mother gave me in life and in gaining linguistic skills. She taught me to be strong, to be a survivor, and to treat others fairly. I am most thankful for my fine teachers all along my educational path and for the wonderful friends and co-workers I was able to accumulate throughout my lifetime. Special thanks to the Rivard family members who were there for me when I needed them.

Were you ever in a bad accident or a long illness?

Luckily, I have been able to sidestep any bad accidents thus far. I have had surgery many times for various things, including back and breast surgery two separate times. Going through radiation afterwards (two different long sessions, totaling around 80 exposures) was not fun. I was lucky to have learned about a doctor with natural leanings who got me through the tiring, grueling weeks by recommending supplements and the natural approach, which my radiologist knew nothing about.

Is there a book or author who helped your philosophy of living?

When I first learned about John Irving and read his novels, it was as if he were writing about life itself. Things go along fine for a while—even quite joyfully, when—BAM! something disastrous happens to remind us of the fragility and brevity of life. In August, 2010, after losing Brian in February, I learned about Michael Perry from Gene Deisz, one of dad's classmates. Gene had brought the little lemon trees he started with some of the seeds we had from the lemons from Brian's tree out in California. Gene was leaving, then casually mentioned that his wife had just read this book about first responders from New Auburn. My ears perked right up, of course, as I had worked in New Auburn during the summer of 1959 and had lived as a kid in the same county. I did some research, found the book, Population: 485 by Michael Perry, ordered it, and have been a devotee ever since, reading everything I can get my hands on that he has written. I was enchanted by Michael's superlative and lyrical use of language, his humble demeanor, his wit and humor, and his very extensive vocabulary. Michael has written about dire things that have happened in his own family and that may lead to helping others to heal from their own sorrows. His honest and elegant writing has certainly helped me. I like to read things by writers who are on a very high spiritual plane and who write about real things.

Before we lost Brian, did tragedy ever strike our family?

My family has had more than its share of bad luck. When I was in college, Gladie lost her only son by drowning in Upper Michigan. She also lost her second husband, Lenard, who was very nice, also by drowning, near where they lived in Grandview. When her grandson (and adopted son), Billy, was about 18, a "friend" pushed him off of a 50 foot cliff in Sturgeon Bay because Billy wouldn't use butane with him. Billy was in a coma for over a year and is now disabled. He retained his great sense of humor, though, and his impeccable manners. My sister, Irene, lost her eldest son in his 40's from a heart attack, and our cousin, Pat, also lost her only son around that same age of the same thing. Our own family has had its share of tribulations, too; but not as much as Gladie. Most families have crosses to bear and heartaches to endure.

Are there still some things you would like to learn to do?

It would be nice to learn to play a musical instrument other than the drums or tonette. Learning to play an Irish lap harp has been on my lengthy "to do" or "bucket" list for a long time. Maybe I could learn to play Brian's guitar one day. I taught myself to knit, and I would like to go beyond the chain stitch in crocheting. One of my friends used to do latch hook rugs; and I would like to try that one day, too. I hope that I continue to learn to be a better gardener and do that all of my life, for "when you have a garden, you have a future, and when you have a future, you have a life".

What goals or ambitions did you have for your life?

In no particular order, with an asterisk by those accomplished: *get out of poverty, *act or do work in theater, *become refined, *do something worthwhile in my life, *have a family, do some serious writing, learn more about watercolor painting, (which I have begun), *never stop learning and reading, *try to stay healthy, *maintain important friendships, *be a grandma, *work with little kids as long as possible, read most significant works (working on it), learn to play the Irish lap harp, *become a gourmet cook, get back to quilting, *learn to knit, learn to crochet, *establish a scholarship, garden as long as possible (still going), volunteer again somewhere worthwhile.

What would you do differently if you could?

Not much. In spite of it all, I have been incredibly blessed. If I could have foretold, and thus forestalled, tragedies in our family, I would have done that. My mother's family seems to have been cursed with tragic loss of the young men in the family, including two of my mother's brothers, sons of two of my sisters, the heartbreaking loss of my own son, numerous miscarriages of male fetuses, one crib death, severe disabilities, and heartache that remains. Among all of these males, Brian's only child, our granddaughter, is lost to us by virtue of having been taken out of the country and out of our lives with no contact at all because the state of California does not think that grandparents have any rights regarding their grandchildren. Sad, when senseless laws take precedence over common sense and family connections.

What would be your most treasured possession?

The most precious things to me cannot be possessed because they are my sons and grandchildren. Of anything material, however, I have a magnificent Baume & Mercier watch, a ring Gene gave me on our 30th anniversary, earrings, and Mikimoto pearl bracelet from Bailey, Banks & Biddle that Gene gave me that I wear all the time. I also have a gorgeous mohair and cashmere German made jacket that I found (never been worn) at a re-sale shop that I wear every chance I get in the fall. My favorite large treasured item is my 10 year old (though still looks new) platinum blue with parchment interior Mercedes Benz E-320 that Brian gave me a year and a half before he was killed. Brian saw the car on a dealer's lot next to his bike trail and checked into it for me. The car had come off lease through a car auction in Anaheim, priced well below its value and ended up in East Palo Alto; we had it shipped by car carrier to Sycamore. When I told Brian that I didn't need a Mercedes, he said: "Well, if you don't drive one now, when will you?" I remember Brian (and take him with me in spirit) every time I drive to my beloved Wisconsin.

What charities do you support?

I am a strong supporter of the University in River Falls. I donate to the theater department, the Blanche Davis scholarship, and the Beverly and William G. Larsen scholarship, in addition to my mother's that I established. I also like the work that the Smile Train does because they work with children to repair cleft lips and palates. Every year, I volunteer for the house walk in Sycamore. Someday, I would like to help in a hospital.

Are all of your siblings still alive?

As I write this, it is amazing that we are all still alive. We are between the ages of 77 and 62. Most of us have health issues, however; but I guess that's to be expected. One sibling has Parkinson's, one has ALS, all of us women have had cancer, some more than once, one has osteoporosis, and many of us have heart issues. I learned through a PET scan or an MRI when I was going through radiation that I have a problem with my subclavian vein and that the collateral vessels have taken over its job. That may explain my short endurance span that has bothered me all my life.

What happened to Grandma B. after all of you were taken away?

We always kept in touch with our mother and each other. My mother worked various jobs as a babysitter, caregiver, nurses' aide in the nursing home in Rib Mountain, as a shelf stocker in the small grocery store in Boyd, and as a maid. She lived in a number of places, including an apartment on Grand Avenue in Chippewa Falls in the building that used to be a hotel. That was very handy for her as she was right down town and could walk to get her yarn and other craft items and to the restaurant next door, called Lindsay's that served excellent food. She developed frontal lobe dementia and when she could no longer care for herself, and needed supervision taking her medications and cleaning herself and her apartment, she had to be placed in the Chippewa Manor nursing home. That was a good placement for her; though it was sad that all of us were far away and could not care for her ourselves.

What happened to Grandma B's land?

It's unfortunate that Grandma's land was sold without consultation or knowledge of eight of us siblings. One of the younger siblings sold the land to a man our mother did not like. The money, we understand, was used for a hair transplant for someone not part of our family. The rest of us thought that the land would always be there as a memorial to our mother's hard work. It ought to have remained in her name in perpetuity. We older siblings, perhaps, had more direct contact with the land so it meant more to us than it did to the younger ones. In addition, someone other than our mother raised the younger ones, so they didn't get the same values instilled in them that our mother gave us older ones. There is a home now on the big north lots and a duplex on the south portion of our mother's land. The people living there, no doubt, have absolutely no idea of the sacrifices and suffering once attached to this very special piece of Mother Earth.

Do you have some tips on living you can share with us?

After getting a good education, I would suggest these: Don't waste things, be kind and polite, lead a productive life, take time to read and learn, don't gossip, live a full, rich life, have children while young, don't put off for tomorrow what you can get done today, maintain friendships, keep in touch—make that call, smile—it's the best accessory, choose a profession in which you can make a difference, keep kids in your life, it's okay to dream and use time in creating, it pays to be neat and clean, always try new things, make the most of the talents and gifts you were blessed with, time is precious—don't kill it, choose positive people to be around, have a garden—then you have a future, leave the world a better place than it was when you came into it.

Imago Animi Sermo Est "Speech Is The Mirror Of The Mind" Seneca (5 BC-65 AD)

Bev & sons on balcony, Montego Bay, Jamaica, 1972

On train ride into the Blue Mountains, Jamaica, 1972.

Gene & sons on balcony.
Note Brendan on floor in infant seat, in use at that time

Georgetown, Grand Cayman, 1974

Richard & Bev, Sycamore, early 70s. Corn was one of his favorite foods

Our family in Glenwood City, approximately 1975.
To left are Michelle with her son, Paul, Ray, Mary & Richard

Under the sea grapes, Grand Cayman, 1976

Andre` cutting Brian's hair, early 70s on porch, Glenwood City

Richard and Brian cutting grass, pool in background

All four sons at Rivard play set next to pool/sauna; house in background

Brian in California (Volkswagen years, early 2000s)

March, 1970, family wedding, Chicago;
L to R: Aunt Laura, Bev, my mother, Louis

Richard and Gene & sons splitting logs

Brian up on sauna by pool, mid-1980s

Brian stoking the sauna, early 1970s

My mother with sons, Brendan is a newborn, November, 1971

Our family by Rudi Achilles, fall, 1978

Napa Valley picnic, late 70s

Our small pool about to be filled, 1972

Friends Tom & Lindy and us by pool

Tom & Lindy with Brian at pool

Bev's retirement from full-time work

Brian & Mary by Richard's homemade bar-b-que area

Brian jumping into pool, Darren by water return